THE FIRST WORLD WAR I~~N~~ ......RAPHS

7

McCUTCHEON

AMBERLEY

First published 2014

Amberley Publishing
The Hill, Stroud
Gloucestershire, GL5 4EP

www.amberley-books.com

British Library Cataloguing in Publication Data.
A catalogue record for this book is available from the British Library.

ISBN 978 1 4456 2210 1 (print)
ISBN 978 1 4456 2226 2 (ebook)

Typeset in 11pt on 15pt Sabon.
Typesetting and Origination by Amberley Publishing.
Printed in the UK.

Contents

A German Army photographer. Note the long lens on the camera.

Introduction –
Russia Revolts and America Finally Enters the War

1917 is dominated by the Russian Revolution and America entering the war. January, however, begins with a massing of troops in Egypt for a push into the Sinai. Between 8 and 9 January, the British troops begin their push to force the Turks out of the Sinai Peninsula. Some 1,600 Turkish troops are captured at the Battle of Magruntein. Only 487 British casualties occur. The invasion of Palestine is planned and the first objectives are the Turkish-held ridges that stretch from Gaza to the Mediterranean. Both British and German fleets resolutely remain in port. Minesweepers combat the menace of mines, with many being lost. Many railway ships are called up for minesweeping duty, and the navy constructs a series of paddle minesweepers named after racecourses. The steam-powered submarine K13 sinks on her trials voyage on 19 January 1917 after her engine room is flooded while diving. Salvaged, she enters service as K22 in March. K4 runs aground in January off Walney Island, Barrow-in-Furness. Also on 19 January, Germany's ambassador in Mexico is sent a message from the German Foreign Minister suggesting a military alliance with the Mexicans. President Woodrow Wilson tries to broker 'peace without victory' on 22 January. The proposal is rejected by the British and French, who cannot agree to some of the German demands. For the past ten months, General John Pershing has been chasing Mexican rebels, including Pancho Villa, with 4,800 troops and he is recalled to the USA on 27 January.

On 3 February, America cuts diplomatic ties with Germany following the announcement on 31 January that Germany will begin unrestricted submarine warfare against the Allies. All 111 U-boats are ordered to sink any vessel at will. The hope is that Britain will be starved into submission as a result. 'All ships will be stopped with every available weapon and without further notice' is the note passed to American Secretary of State Robert Lansing. It is estimated by the Germans that if America declares war it will take up to two years for American troops to have an impact, by which time the Central Powers will have gained victory. As Woodrow Wilson, America's President, says in a speech that 'this government has no alternative consistent with the dignity and honour of the United States' and cuts diplomatic ties, a German U-boat sinks the American steamer *Housatonic*.

· in the West is quiet as the winter continues but on 22 February, the Middle East hots up. General Sir Frederick Maude pushes his troops s towards Baghdad. A major attack at Kut-el-Amara sees the Turks abandon the city by 25 February and retreat towards Baghdad. On the Western Front, the Germans have almost completed their Hindenburg Line and begin the two-month-long retreat towards it on 23 February. The new Hindenburg Line is some 20 miles from the existing front but tidies up many extraneous parts of the front, making it shorter and easier to defend. As they retreat back, the Germans operate a scorched earth policy, destroying towns and villages, cutting down forests and poisoning the available water supplies. By 5 April, the retreat is complete and the new line stretches from Arras to Soissons. The US Ambassador to the United Kingdom is given a copy of a message written by the German Foreign Minister, Arthur Zimmermann, that proposes that Mexico should enter the war if America declares war on Germany. The uproar created in the USA is massive and turns many Americans who may have supported Germany against them.

On 8 March, Germany is boosted as the Russians begin to demonstrate against shortages of food and fuel. Revolution is in the air! Riots, strikes and huge demonstrations break out in Moscow. The police shoot at the demonstrators but the protests continue. By 10 March, 25,000 workers are on strike and army units refuse to shoot at the protesters. With the Russians using a different calendar, the protests become known as the February Revolution. The Russian leader, Tzar Nicholas II, is asked by the Duma, Russia's Parliament, on 11 March to make urgent political reforms but ignores them and orders the disbanding of the Duma, which refuses and still meets in an increasingly lawless Petrograd. Baghdad is entered on 11 March as the Iraqi capital falls to force while the Russian capital disintegrates into anarchy on 12 March. Left-wing activists, protesters and politicians form the Petrograd Soviet. Its first order is to relieve Russian officers of their responsibilities and by 14 March a provisional government is formed. During the chaos, the army refuses to prevent the spread of revolution and the Germans do not help by sending revolutionary leader Vladimir Lenin back to Russia in a sealed train.

The Americans announce on 13 March that they will be arming all US merchant ships in areas where U-boats are known to operate. Tzar Nicholas abdicates on 15 March and the revolution gathers momentum. On the 17th, German destroyers sink two British destroyers and a merchant ship. The next day, three American vessels, the *City of Memphis*, *Vigilancia* and *Illinois*, are sunk by U-boat, despite showing neutral colours. It is this that brings America closer to war. The invasion of Palestine begins on 26 March with 16,000 Allied troops attacking through the Gaza–Beersheba line. Turkish resistance, a lack of water and poor communications see the day end with 2,500 Turkish casualties and 4,000 British. Yet another hospital ship is sunk on 31 March. HMHS *Gloucester Castle* is hit off the Isle of Wight by a torpedo from UB-32 but is salvaged.

2 April sees Wilson address Congress, citing the German submarine warfare, the loss of three ships on the one day and the Zimmermann telegram as nothing less

Above: A British fighter pilot fixes an ammunition drum on his machine gun.

than war on the USA. Congress has basically been asked to go to war. As America readies for war, Vladimir Lenin arrives back in Petrograd on 3 April. His intention is no less than overthrowing the Provisional Government to create a state run by the Bolsheviks. On 6 April, the United States declares war on Germany. The US Navy is much better prepared than the army, which needs to be expanded, and quickly. Wilson sees this as a moral crusade and decides not to become a full ally of the British, French and Russians. He basically wants to stop the war and does not want to get involved in the politics of Europe. Three days later, the spring offensives begin on the Western Front with the Battle of Arras. The plan is to make the Germans withdraw troops from the Aisne, where the French are about to open an offensive. Three British armies attack at Arras with the middle of them attacking Arras itself, the northern army trying to take Vimy Ridge, and in the south the army attacking Bullecourt. The attack begins with a five-day bombardment and the first day of the battle sees large gains for the British and Canadian troops. Vimy Ridge is captured and some 4 miles of enemy ground are taken but the area around Bullecourt sees few advances. The Royal Flying Corps suffers too with fully a third of all British fighter pilots becoming casualties in April. Their aircraft are no match for the German Albatross D.III or the German pilots' tactics of diving onto the British aircraft and catching them unawares. On 11 April, the British consolidate gains and break into the Hindenburg Line at Bullecourt but the battle is beginning to turn the same way as every other battle on the Western Front in the past year: a stalemate. The battle has to continue though, not because of the chance of success, but to keep the Germans from pushing into the French lines. The French soldiers

Above: Negotiating the mud on duck-board walkways. *Below:* Dead horses lie amid the debris of the battle scene at Pilkem. Thousands of horses were killed on the Western Front.

have been mutinying and their leadership is in disarray. By the time the offensive ends in May, 100,000 Germans are dead or wounded with 150,000 British and Canadian troops killed, wounded or captured.

The troopship *Arcadian* is sunk by UC-74 in the southern Aegean on the night of 15 April with the loss of some 277. Over 1,000 crew and troops are rescued. The French open an offensive between 16 and 20 April along the Aisne river and in the Champagne region. 7,000 French artillery pieces and 102,000 soldiers face two German armies and attack along a 40-mile front between Soissons and Rheims. Unfortunately for the French, the Germans are aware of their plans and destroy many of the French balloons used for spotting for their artillery. The French troops advance into well-defended positions and a huge German artillery barrage. By 20 April, 118,000 French soldiers are dead or wounded and it is obvious that the offensive will not capture its planned objectives. The fighting continues into May but with little success and more casualties. The day after the offensive begins, troops of the French 108th Regiment mutiny and abandon their trenches. Soon, men of sixty-eight of France's 112 divisions are involved, with officers reporting 250 examples of troops refusing to obey orders. Some 35,000 men are implicated in the mutiny, with many defending their trenches but refusing to advance against the enemy. Another attempt is made to break the Turkish lines in Palestine between 17 and 19 April. The British casualties reach 6,500 against well-defended Turkish positions. No more than 2,500 Turks become casualties. 20–21 April sees a German incursion into the English Channel. Fortunately, the destroyers *Broke* and *Swift* see them off and the daring Channel raids stop. On 23 April an attack by British Handley Page O/100 bombers is made on a flotilla of German torpedo boats at Ostend. Several of the boats are damaged but losses over the coming weeks see daylight raids like this stop. In Iraq, the British advance takes Samarra on 23 April but the summer heat sees all operations cease till September.

The French introduce their first tank, the St Chamond, on 5 May. The St Chamond has a crew of nine, with four machine guns and a 75-mm main gun. Unreliable and plagued with mechanical problems, some 400 are built. Albert Ball, who had won a Victoria Cross in the skies above France, is killed on 7 May.

On 7–8 May, British forces bombard the Belgian port of Zeebrugge, from where many U-boats operate. The French offensive along the Chemin des Dames finishes in failure on 9 May. 187,000 French have died or been wounded! 163,000 Germans have died, been wounded or captured. It is these rates of attrition for no benefit that make the French soldiers question their leaders' abilities and that have led to mutiny. French soldiers are deployed in the Salonika front, in the Balkans, too. On 9 May, as one offensive ends, another begins half a continent away as Serbian and French troops attack in Macedonia. The French and Serbians attack across the Vardar river, with the British attacking around Lake Doiran. The offensive achieves little apart from 14,000 Allied casualties. May also sees the convoy system in operation. At the beginning of the war, troopships in convoy had brought many thousands of Canadians, Australians and New Zealanders to Britain but the practice had ceased. Losses to submarines were now so great that

Britain is in danger of running out of food and the convoy system is brought back. The impact is huge and German U-boat losses climb rapidly. On 12 May, General Pershing is made commander of the American Expeditionary Force. His intention is to bring a million troops to Europe by May 1918. Pershing will arrive in Liverpool aboard White Star's *Baltic* on 24 June. On the Western Front, the Tenth Battle of the Isonzo begins on 12 May. In a seventeen-day-long battle, the Italians yet again fail to make headway and lose 160,000 men, with the Austro-Hungarians losing around 75,000. On 15 May, Austro-Hungarian ships attack Italian vessels off the Albanian coast. Before British, Italian and French warships can intervene, fourteen ships are sunk. The leader of the daring raid is Captain Miklos Horthy, who will later become dictator of Hungary. The French commander-in-chief is sacked on 15 May and replaced by General Pétain, who quells the mutinous French soldiers after numerous visits to the Front to talk with them. Fifty are executed for mutiny though. London is bombed by land-based aircraft for the first time on 23 May when sixteen Gotha bombers attack London from Belgium. They miss London but drop bombs on a Canadian camp, killing 100 soldiers.

At the beginning of June the Russians change their chief of staff but their war is nearly over. 7 June sees another British offensive on the Western Front at the Messines Ridge. The ridge needs to be captured so that a hoped-for offensive to break the German lines at Ypres can take place. Since the last week in May, British artillery pieces had been bombarding the German lines. Underneath their trenches, the British had mined the land. Tunneling underneath the lines, huge quantities of explosives are placed and detonated in massive explosions. A day of heavy

On 12 May 1917, General John 'Black Jack' Pershing, shown left, was made commander of the new American Expeditionary Force going to fight in France. He arrived in Europe in June to oversee the build-up of the US forces, which would reach 2 million men by the end of the war. Pershing was a controversial figure and his reliance on costly frontal attacks, even after the other protagonists had abandoned such tactics, has been criticised for causing high casualties among the US troops.

fighting sees 17,500 casualties but the Messines Ridge is captured. 25,000 German casualties include 7,500 prisoners. The day's work makes the future Third Battle of Ypres possible.

An unusual feat of salvage is undertaken when the bow of the destroyer *Zulu* is mated with the stern of the *Nubian* to create the *Zubian*, which enters service on 7 June. She is scrapped in 1919. Gotha bombers attack London again on 13 June, causing 104 deaths and wounding 400. Anti-aircraft guns are placed around the city and cause the Germans to move to nighttime raids. The first American troops land in Liverpool on 24 June and it will be the start of a build-up that will see 180,000 troops in Europe by the end of the year. The Greeks, who have seen King Constantine abdicate on 12 June, enter the war against the Central Powers on 27 June.

The Russians are still fighting in the East and 1 July will see a huge offensive from them, but their days of war are numbered. The Kerensky offensive begins with an attack against Lemberg using the Russian Eleventh, Eighth and Seventh armies. With revolution at home, the ordinary Russian soldiers, while still fighting, are beginning to show signs of unrest and the offensive's advances stop. At Scapa Flow, on the evening of 9 July 1917, HMS *Vanguard* explodes. The St Vincent Class battleship was built in 1909 and it is thought that cordite had overheated and caused an explosion near turrets P and Q. Only two crew survived the explosion and 804 men lost their lives. Included among the dead was a Japanese naval observer, Captain Kyosuke Eto. Pieces of metal that landed on HMS *Bellerophon* were from the dynamo room, which suggested that the explosion had been in the centre of the ship.

A British air offensive begins over Ypres on 11 July, as the British hope to push the Germans from the skies before their next offensive at Passchendaele. On 18 July, the artillery offensive begins using 1,400 guns to drop hundreds of thousands of gas and high explosive shells around Ypres. The shelling pounds the ground, leaving it pock-marked with craters, and totally destroys the drainage, causing problems that will hamper the British as they advance. The German parliament reaches an agreement for peace that basically agrees with that proposed by President Woodrow Wilson on 19 July. On the same day, the Germans launch a counteroffensive against the Russians. With many Russians refusing to fight, the Germans make good their losses of land since the Kerensky offensive started. The Serbian government in exile agrees to unite the various groups from the Serbs and Slovenes to Croats and Montenegrins to form the united state of Yugoslavia on 20 July. The trial of Margaretha Zelle begins on 24 July. Under her stage name of Mata Hari, the Dutch national is accused of espionage for the Germans. Dubious evidence does not stop her being executed later in the year. At the end of the month, the Germans reorganise their air force, creating large wings with some fifty or so aircraft. With its aircraft painted in bright colours, the most famous is Richthofen's Flying Circus. The bombardment has ceased at Ypres and the Third Battle of Ypres begins on 31 July. The plan that has been building since the capture of the Vimy Ridge is to smash through the German armies, and to venture a few miles up the coast and turn to capture Ostend and Zeebrugge. Once these two German submarine and destroyer bases were captured, the Allies would throw the Germans out of Belgium. Initial British gains are not as good as expected, and the Allies reach 2 miles into German-held territory.

On 2 August 1917, Squadron Commander Edwin Dunning successfully landed a Sopwith Pup on board HMS *Furious*, becoming the first person to land an aircraft on a moving ship. The aircraft carrier had come of age. Changes of leadership in the Russian army are intended to prevent the Russian army from disintegrating. The Battle of Ypres is suspended due to torrential rain, which turns the churned-up land into a muddy swamp. On 16 August, the battle recommences as the flooded ground dries out. The Germans have had time to reinforce their lines and their heavy resistance, plus a still muddy terrain, cause the offensive to falter after a few hundred yards. On 17 August, it is proposed that the Royal Flying Corps and Royal Naval Air Service amalgamate to become the Royal Air Force. This will have an impact post-war on the Navy's aircraft carriers, which will become the dominant naval weapon of the next war. A day later, the Italians attempt once more to attack in the Isonzo, in what becomes known as the Eleventh Battle of the Isonzo. Fifty-two divisions and 5,000 guns face the Austro-Hungarians. For once the Italians make gains in the north but in the south they are again held

Below: German prisoners taken in the Arras offensive, 9–16 May 1917. The assault is noteworthy for the extensive use of tunnels to take Commonwealth troops under German lines.

by the Austro-Hungarians. The Austro-Hungarians are near collapse and have to call the Germans in for reinforcements. Italian losses are 166,000 and the Austro-Hungarians lose 85,000 in the battle, which finishes on 15 September.

An offensive against Riga by the Germans begins on 1 September. Hoping to take some ground as the Russian defence falls apart, the attack begins with a short bombardment then attacks by highly trained storm troopers, who are supported by mobile artillery. The Dvina is soon crossed and the Russian Twelfth Army collapses. Between 9 and 14 September, a coup is attempted in Russia against the Bolsheviks by General Lavr Kornilov but it fails. On the Western Front, the focus of the fighting at Ypres moves to the south and to the ridges there. General Sir Herbert Plummer's plan is to take bit-sized chunks at a time until the ridges have been captured. A series of battles ensue: Menin Road (20–25 September), Polygon Wood (26 September) and Broodseinde (4 October). For once, this slow approach works, despite the Germans' use of mustard gas for the first time. The ground has dried out and this aids the advance, but by the end of the battles it has become waterlogged again after heavy rain. On the air front, German ace Werner Voss (forty-eight kills) is killed by British pilots led by James McCudden, who will take fifty-seven kills before he himself dies in 1918. At the end of September the battle in Mesopotamia continues and between 27 and 28 September, the British advance north along the Euphrates. The meet and fight the Turks at Ramadi and the British chase the defeated Turks, who head towards Mosul.

Between 9 and 12 October, the British change their focus at Ypres back to the north-east of the town. The Australian troops committed fail to make much progress and it is painfully obvious that the British will not achieve their objectives before winter sets in. However, Field Marshal Haig orders an attack around Passchendaele on 12 October but it fails. An attack on a convoy from Scandinavia of fourteen ships with two escorts, HMS *Mary Rose* and *Strongbow*, on 17 October sees the German cruisers *Bremse* and *Brummer* sink both destroyers and sink the majority of the merchant vessels. The Battle of Moon Sound on the same day sees the Russian battleship *Slava* sunk. Eventually salvaged, she lasted until 1935.

Three of eleven German Zeppelin airships are destroyed in a raid on Britain on 19 October. It is not the British air force that destroys them but the weather. Another is shot down by ground fire and a fifth simply disappears. Of the remaining six, all fail to reach their targets and are either captured or crash in enemy territory. This is the last major Zeppelin rain on the UK and the airships are then used to support the German navy.

The Twelfth Battle of the Isonzo opens on 24 October with an Austro-Hungarian offensive and shelling of the Italians. Gas and high explosive shells rain down on the Italians. With German reinforcements, the Austro-Hungarians attack a prepared Italian defence. However, the shelling causes panic in the Italian lines, as the Italians discover that their gas masks are no help against the poison gas. A 15-mile front is opened up and the Italians retreat on 27 October to the river Tagliamento. Brazil declares war on Germany on 26 October after a series of Brazilian merchant ships are sunk by U-boats. It is the only South American

THE DANCE OF DEATH.

The Kaiser: 'Stop! Stop! I'm tired.' Death: 'I started at your bidding; I stop when I choose.' *Punch* cartoon, published in October 1917.

country to declare war. Passchendaele is attacked once more on 26 October and the battle continues until 10 November. The use of mustard gas and the treacherous conditions underfoot have slowed the progress but the village is finally taken on 10 November. This battle, beginning in July, has cost 310,000 British troops to take some 5 miles of front. The supporting French troops have lost 85,000 and the Germans have got off lightly with 260,000 casualties. On 27 October a young German officer called Erwin Rommel, using 250 highly trained mountain troops, captures some 9,000 Italians during the Battle of Caporetto. In Palestine, on 31 October, British troops launch the Third Battle of Gaza. Camel corps are included among the 88,000 Allied troops who attack the Gaza–Beersheba line once more. A feint attack is launched against the Turks at Gaza while Allenby's main force attacks Beersheba and its vital water supply. Only 35,000 Turks face the British and Commonwealth force and the battle is won by the Australian cavalry, who charge through the Turkish defences and take Beersheba. The Turks are forced into retreat and weaken the Turkish armies on the coast, exposing their flank to the Allies.

Britain's Foreign Secretary, Arthur Balfour, writes what becomes known as the Balfour Declaration to the chairman of the British Zionist Federation, which supports the creation of an independent Jewish state in the Middle East. This letter, written on 2 November, also expresses a desire to protect the rights of the Arabs and Christians in Palestine too. The Germans fighting in Italy force the crossing of the river Tagliamento during darkness on the night of 2 November, breaking the new defensive line the Italians have created. They abandon their lines and make a new defensive stand at the Piave river, which they complete by 9 November.

The Americans, who are now arriving in France in huge quantities, suffer their first three casualties on 3 November. After the huge Italian defeat the Allies create a Supreme War Council on 5 November. The next day, Allenby consolidates his wins at Beersheba and sends his Desert Mounted Corps towards Gaza. The Turkish Eighth Army retreats from Gaza and the defeated Seventh Army heads for Jerusalem. In Russia, the revolution continues and the Bolsheviks seize power and overthrow the Provisional Government. They quickly begin discussions with the Germans about an armistice. The fighting on the Isonzo front stops on 12 November as the Germans and Austro-Hungarians have overstretched their supply lines. The battle has been disastrous for the Allies with the loss of 275,000 Italians captured by the Central Powers. 30,000 have died or been seriously wounded. The Central Powers have captured 2,500 artillery weapons as well as huge quantities of materiel, all for the loss of only 20,000 soldiers. A new front has been created and the huge numbers of men killed in twelve battles have been for nothing as the Italians have lost ground, despite taking the offensive in so many of the twelve battles. British troops are soon rushed to Italy to support the faltering troops. The battle has been brought to Italy and figures like Benito Mussolini encourage Italians to fight for their country. In the Middle East, Allenby's troops are chasing the Turks in Palestine. At Junction Station, a site of much needed water for both sides, between 13 and 15 November, a battle is fought that sees the Allied troops break through the Turkish defences and head towards Jerusalem. A German Zeppelin, L59, has been sent to East Africa to supply General Paul von Lettow-Vorbeck's troops but is ordered to turn back on 17 November as Germany fears Lettow-Vorbeck is about to surrender. In Iraq, the British commander, General Maude, dies of cholera on 18 November. He is buried near Baghdad. General Sir Julian Byng leads the attack in what is known as the Battle of Cambrai, which sees tanks used in huge numbers. Some 476 tanks are used by the British as they try to punch a hole in the Hindenburg Line between the Canal de l'Escaut and the Canal du Nord. The battle opens with a barrage by 1,000 guns. The first attacks are hugely successful, and the Hindenburg Line is breached to a depth of 8 miles in parts. Only at Flesquières is the advance halted as the Germans knock out many tanks and the British co-ordination between infantry and tanks is woefully lacking. Despite initial successes, the momentum is hard to keep up and the advance becomes bogged down as tanks succumb to German fire and mechanical breakdown. Despite many carrying fascines to cross trenches and ditches, the tanks become stuck and are destroyed by German artillery. The Germans counter-attack and the fighting continues into December. In East Africa, the outnumbered Germans under Lettow-Vorbeck retreat into Portuguese East Africa. With the Allies closing in from all sides, the Germans lose about a third of their army on the 27th. However, they continue to fight until the war's end in a guerilla campaign that sees many thousands of Allied troops (mainly Indian and British) tied up. On 30 November, a German counteroffensive at Cambrai sees attempts to regain lost territory. These are highly successful due to a change in German tactics: a short barrage, followed by the use of storm troopers and coordinated air support. The over-extended Allied troops are pushed back and lose most of their gains over the coming days.

December sees the Russians and Germans discuss peace terms at Brest-Litovsk. An armistice has been put in place but these discussions will see the end to the war in the east. At Cambrai, the British have lost 40,000 men, the same as the Germans, with around 10,000 prisoners on each side. Many tanks captured by the Germans at Cambrai are moved behind the lines to be pressed into service for the Central powers. Both sides have learned something from Cambrai though. Huge artillery bombardments are not needed to see victory, and the use of tanks in the numbers seen at Cambrai can lead to a swift advance. We shall see the results in the offensives of 1918. The Americans declare war on Austria-Hungary on 7 December. Cossacks in Russia revolt against the Bolsheviks on 9 December and the Turks abandon Jerusalem. Allenby enters the ancient city on 11 December. The Japanese invade Vladivostock on 30 December. Further revolution in Russia has seen the Cossacks revolt against the Bolsheviks and British ships shell the Bolsheviks.

And so ends 1917! The naval war has increased in intensity, America enters the war and Russia is a spent force. The fifth year of the war, 1918, will bring new trials and tribulations for both sides.

JANUARY 1917

The effect of the war spread among all strata of society. At a school in Bradford these boys are shown making boxes for soldiers' parcels. Some of the war work undertaken by children had a far greater impct upon their education and it is estimated that by 1917 around 600,000 children had been withdrawn prematurely from school and immersed in industry. They were put to work on the land, in munitions factories and even in the mines.

A PLAIN DUTY.

"WELL, GOODBYE, OLD CHAP, AND GOOD LUCK! I'M GOING IN HERE TO DO MY BIT, THE BEST WAY I CAN. THE MORE EVERYBODY SCRAPES TOGETHER FOR THE WAR LOAN, THE SOONER YOU'LL BE BACK FROM THE TRENCHES."

This *Punch* cartoon on 'The Great War Loan' was published on 7 February 1917.

War Loans

On the Home Front, doing your bit often meant putting your hand in your pocket to help finance the costly business of the on-going war. On 11 January 1917 the British Prime Minister, David Lloyd George, launched a patriotic appeal for the nation to subscribe to the new War Loan. By this time the cost of the war was running at over £5 million a day. The 5 per cent loan was for thirty years, and the 4 per cent loan ran for twenty-five years, tax-free. The promise was that the loan would shorten the war and 'save the lives of the brave young men at the Front'.

Other nations also called upon the public to finance the war. Shown above, Parisians examine war loan notices outside the Bank of France. *Right:* 1917 poster for the Sixth War Loan in Austria-Hungary. Designed by Maximilian Lenz, it features the familiar figure of St George killing the dragon and mimics an almost identical British poster. More posters are shown overleaf.

A selection of British posters emphasising the need to invest in the War Loan to feed the almost insatiable appetite of the war machine. In the end, it was the industrial might and resources of the combatants that would eventually decide the outcome of this long drawn-out war.

Above: The K-class submarines were designed in 1913 as a means of providing the main battle fleets with submarines that could keep up with them. The steam-powered submarines started coming into service in late 1916 and early 1917. K4 is shown ashore at Walney Island, Barrow-in-Furness, in January 1917. None were lost by enemy action but six were lost in accidents, including the 1918 Battle of May Island. *Below:* K26 was ordered as an improved version and the only one of six submarines to be built. She was not scrapped until 1931. The K-class vessels were 339 feet long and, being steam powered, could take up to five minutes to dive.

Above: Train ferries operated out of the military port at Richborough, Kent, taking much-needed supplies to France without the need to unload and reload again.

Above: HMS *Ben-my-Chree* was one of the seaplane carriers taken up for service from British ferries. Originally owned by the Isle of Man Steam Packet Company and built at Barrow for the Liverpool–Isle of Man route, in August 1916 one of her seaplanes dropped the first aerial torpedo against an enemy ship. On 11 January 1917, Turkish guns shelled the *Ben-my-Chree* and sank her. She was salvaged but was a total constructive loss and was scrapped in 1923.

H.M.S. Biarritz, leaving Mudros, 1917.

The SECR ferry *Biarritz* was built by William Denny, of Dumbarton. In March 1915, she was taken over by the Admiralty and commissioned as a minelayer. She is shown at Mudros. At the end of the war, she was handed back over to her owners and used on the Folkestone–Boulogne route. During the Second World War, she was used as an infantry landing ship.

H.M.S. MONA'S ISLE

The Isle of Man Steam Packet Company's *Mona's Isle* as a minesweeper during the war. Note the washing hanging out to dry. Usually stationed at Harwich, she travelled as afar as southern Ireland, where she helped in the recovery of £86,000 of gold from a sunken Dutch steamer.

FEBRUARY 1917

At an advanced dressing station German prisoners help with the stretchers carrying wounded Allied soldiers. It was vital that they were treated as quickly as possible in what was known as the 'race against infection'. As a result, more cases were treated at casualty clearing stations nearer to the firing line in order to eliminate the time spent in taking them to bases located further back. 'Patients began the race with inflammation on good terms and with a reserve of strength. Their wounds were less dangerous, healed quicker and left less permanent damage behind them. They were disabled for a shorter period, and so could be expected back at their duties in a shorter period.'

Many women in Britain were to play their part in the war, carrying out a wide range of duties. *Top:* A route march of the Women's Army Auxiliary Corps in France. The first scheme for the WAACs was launched in 1917. *Bottom:* Women carpenters at work, also in France.

A photograph published in an American magazine to illustrate the essential war work being carried out by British women on the Home Front. Many worked on the trains and buses, keeping the transportation system running, in order to release more men for the fighting.

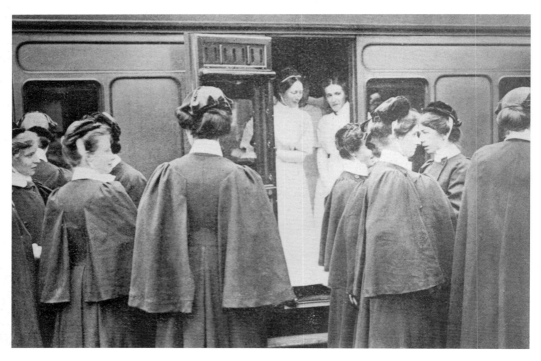

Above: A batch of English nurses entraining at a London station, probably Victoria, for the boat train to France. *Below:* Open-air treatment beside the River Thames for soldiers recuperating at St Thomas's Hospital, opposite the Houses of Parliament.

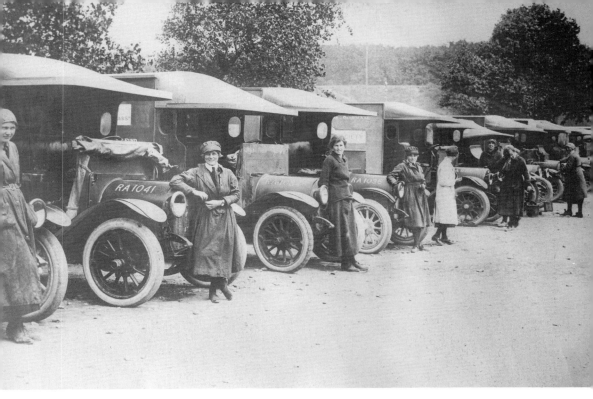

Above: Women ambulance drivers with a line-up of their vehicles in France. All types of vehicles were pressed into service as ambulances. *Below:* A pair of specially equipped motorcyles operated by the Nottingham Corps of the Saint John's Ambulance Brigade are put on display.

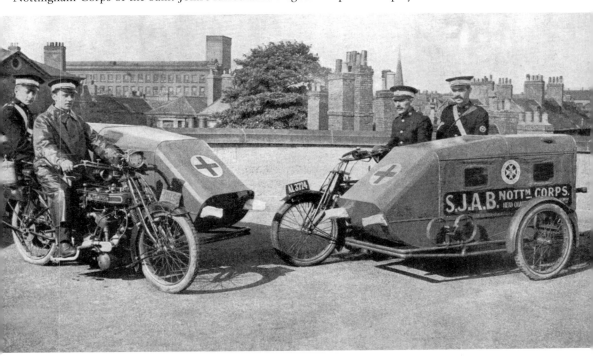

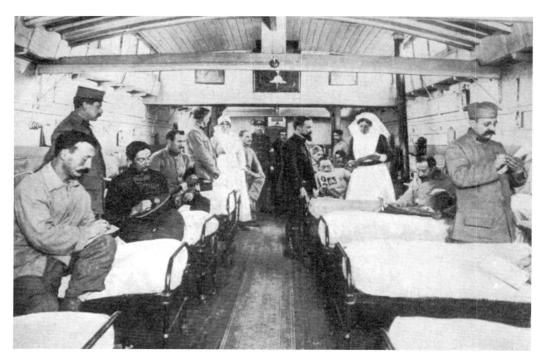

Two photographs of the hospital barges moored on the Seine at one of the quays at Paris. A small fleet of these well-equipped vessels travelled on the French waterways from behind the Allied lines.

Above: An army motor kitchen supplied and operated by the YMCA. Founded in 1844, this charitable organisation supported the troops by supplying food and a place to rest in its special huts, both on the front line, shown below, and at home at military camps and railway stations.

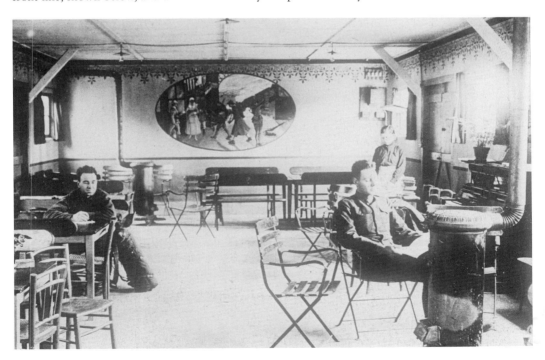

Above: Aerial photograph of the defensive lines at Bullecourt on the Hindenburg Line.

The Hindenburg Line

This defensive line was constructed by the Germans over the winter of 1916/17 in anticipation of an increase in Anglo-French attacks in 1917. The line of earthworks, barbed wire and bunkers was around 20 miles behind the existing front line and ran from Arras up to Laffaux, near Soissons on the Aisne. In the salient between the old front and the new defences the Germans systematically demolished civilian buildings in order to present the advancing Allies with a desert in which the road and rail infrastructure would have to be rebuilt, thus causing a considerable delay. In the process the Germans destroyed whole villages, woodland was cut down and the water supply poisoned. A preliminary withdrawal began at the end of February and the Alberich Bewegung (the 'manoeuvre') continued through March and was completed by early April.

Opposite page: A French woman sits amid the ruins of her home after returning to territory recently abandoned by the Germans in their retreat to the Hindenburg Line.

Despite the damage to the upper storeys of this building, it is business as usual as far as possible, and this French woman sells produce to the troops not far behind the front line.

Above: Life for rural communities in the occupied areas was hard, and these peasant women are forced to pull a plough as their horses have taken by the Germans. *Below:* In contrast, this scene in Paris seems reassuringly normal with the street traders preparing for the day's business.

MARCH 1917

This disabled British tank in Palestine has been stripped of all useful parts and left to rot. There is clear evidence of shell damage to its flanks.

Above: A Turkish supply train moves across the barren landscape of the Sinai Peninsula in Egypt.
Below: British field dressing station in Palestine. The Allies had launched the Third Battle of Gaza
at the end of October 1917.

Above: Shells are lined up in readiness beside a Turkish artillery gun. *Below:* 'Nablus Lizzy', a German-built 15-cm Kanone 16 heavy field gun, shown in Gaza in its transport configuration with the barrel detached.

Above: Another view of the wreck of a knocked-out British tank in Palestine. *Below:* 'Jericho Jane'. This German gun had been used to bombard Jericho and is shown overturned after its capture at the Wadi Nimrin in the spring of 1918.

This page: An Allied burial party stands by the grave of Turkish soldiers who fell at Tell El Fal battlefield, a hill to the east of the Nablus road in Palestine.

Opposite page: One of the fallen Turks, still grasping a German-style stick grenade.

In 1917 revolution was in the air in Russia. *Above:* Bullet holes in a shop window after riots in Petrograd. Known as St Petersburg until 1914, Petrograd was the capital of the Russian Empire at this time and a 'soviet' – a city council – was created following the so-called February Revolution of 1917, although this had taken place from 8 to 12 March according to the modern calander. The capital changed to Moscow at the end of the war, and Petrograd was renamed Leningrad in 1924. It has since reverted to St Petersburg. *Below:* The Provisional Executive Committee of the State Duma. First created in 1905, the elected Duma would have an important role in the abolition of autocracy in Russia.

Troops on the streets of Petrograd in 1917, shown top at the State Duma and, bottom, in the Literny Prospekt, a wide avenue running through the central district of the city.

Tzar Nicholas II, the last emperor of Russia. Following his forced abdication on 15 March 1917, the Tzar was held under arrest at the Alexander Palace in Tsarkoe Selo – the Tzar village – the former summer residence of the imperial family near St Petersburg. The Tzar, above left, and members of his family are shown shovelling snow and working in the gardens of the palace.

Alexei Nikolaevich, Tzarevich, heir to the Russian throne, together with his sister, the Grand Duchess Tatiana, shown at work in the gardens at Tsarkoe Selo.

Above: HMHS *Mauretania* leaving a French port at night, showing the electric lights that helped identify her as a hospital ship. 1917 was a year of atrocities and sinkings and these were what pushed America into war against Germany. *Below:* On 3 March 1917, HMHS *Gloucester Castle*, despite wearing her hospital ship livery, was torpedoed by Kapitänleutnant Max Viebeg's UB-32 off the Isle of Wight. She was salvaged and towed back to port two weeks after the sinking but three died in the transfer of her crew and wounded soldier passengers.

Muirhead Bone had been appointed as the first British Official War Artist by Charles Masterman, the head of the British War Propaganda Bureau. He had arrived in France in August 1916, during the Battle of the Somme, and in addition to his depictions of the action at the Front he also produced a series of images of the hospital ships.

Above: Wounded men being taken aboard a hospital ship. Visible in the centre is the large timber red cross mounted on the side of the ship. The ship would be illuminated with green lights at night. *Right:* Embarking the stretcher cases.

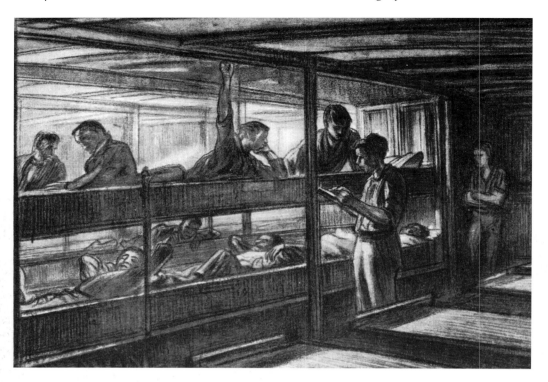

Two more of Muirhead Bone's drawings of hospital ships. *Above:* Tiers of bunks inside a ship. *Below:* The 'walking wounded' find a place to sleep on deck on warm summer nights.

APRIL 1917

Recycling is nothing new! Here, we see some of the crew of HMS *Barham* larking about in 1917. At this stage of the war, nothing was wasted and with the unrestricted submarine warfare and a German blockade of Britain by submarine, these scraps would be recycled.

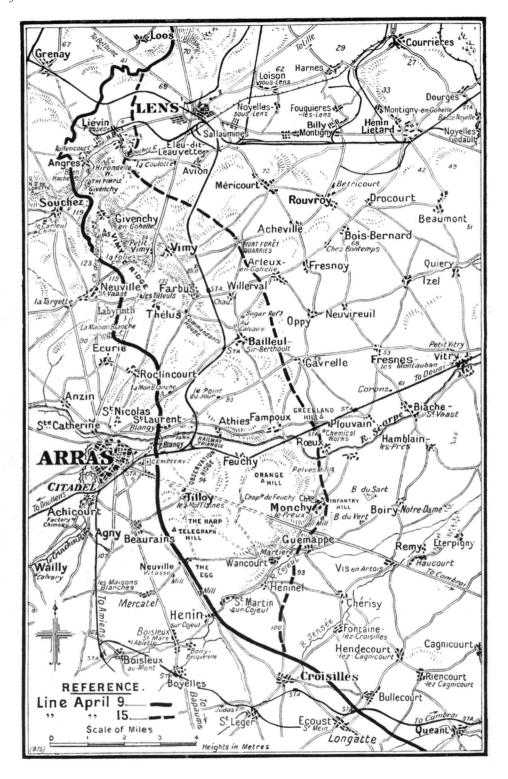

Top: British troops in a corner of the battlefield near Arras. Note the Mark IV in the background. This appears to be a 'tank tender', a gun-less tank used to tow the field guns and deliver supplies. 205 of these were produced in addition to the male and female armed tanks. *Bottom:* British soldiers examining a captured German gun.

Top: A stack of empty shell cases. These would have been collected and returned to the foundries.
Bottom: French troops examine a captured observation post.

British sentries stand guard amid the ruined buildings of Feuchy, a village south of the main road from Arras to Cambrai. See map on page 50.

Above: French soldiers sorting through captured material. *Below:* The stumps of what had been woodland on the heights of Moronvilliers. The village was deserted and destroyed in the war.

The USA Enters the War

On 6 April 1917 the USA finally entered
the war. President Woodrow Wilson,
right, had addressed Congress earlier in
the week, calling upon Americans to go
to war: 'The world must be made safe for
democracy.' The decision represented a
dramatic reversal for the President as he
had resisted the USA's participation in
an attempt to maintain readiness while
facilitating the possibility of a peace
agreement. The USA's entry brought its
manpower and vast industrial might to
bear on the side of the Allies.

Below: Launching of a super dreadnought at a
US Navy shipyard in 1917.

In the first seven months after America's entrance into this war for human freedom, enemy agitators in our midst caused 283,402 workers to lose 6,285,519 days of production. Our war industries were heavily handicapped by this unpatriotic strife.

LET US ALL PULL TOGETHER TO WIN THE WAR QUICKLY

Left and above: Two posters from a series warning of the danger of enemy agitators disrupting output of the US war industries.

Below: Women painters in the camouflaging department of the American Car & Foundry Co., Detroit.

As in Great Britain, the American public was encouraged to subscribe to public loans to finance the war effort. The Secretary of the Treasury, William McAdoo, is shown top addressing a Liberty Loan event in Washington DC. Meanwhile his wife, shown in the foreground in the lower photograph, does her bit by heading the Women's Liberty Loan Committee.

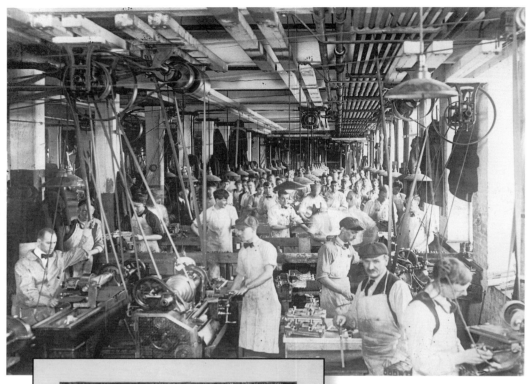

OUR COUNTRY NEEDS SHIPS

to carry our boys "Over There" and keep them well supplied with Food, Clothing and the Munitions of War.

The product made in this plant is used for building ships. The ships can be completed only as fast as the material and equipment for each ship arrives at the shipyard.

If every man does a better day's work every day, the ships can be built faster.

BE TRUE TO THE BOYS WHO ARE GIVING THEIR LIVES FOR YOU

UNITED STATES SHIPPING BOARD EMERGENCY FLEET CORPORATION
ISSUED BY PUBLICATION SECTION, PHILADELPHIA

Above: These impeccably attired workers are producing munitions in a US factory.

Left: Poster reminding Americans that their country needed ships. It might be stating the obvious, but it was vital that the US had an adequate supply of ships to maintain the flow of men and munitions across the Atlantic. 'If every man does a better day's work every day, the ships can be built faster.'

Above: With America in the war, their shipbuilding yards soon began to make up for the losses to submarines that had taken place. American shipyards down both coasts began to build standard designs of vessels. Here, four are being fitted out after launch in an unknown American shipyard. *Below:* Boring a 14-inch gun at a US naval yard.

The monitor *Marshal Soult* spent parts of 1917 bombarding the Flanders coast. She took part in the First Ostend raid in 1918.

HMS *Swift* was designed for speed but failed to reach her contract speed of 36 knots. She was eventually taken up by the navy after numerous attempts to improve her speed. In 1917, she was part of the Dover Patrol and took part in the Battle of Dover Strait on the night of 20/21 April. She hit the German destroyer G65 with a torpedo and HMS *Broke* rammed G42. With these two ships gone, the Germans retreated. The survivors of G42 were rescued and taken to Plymouth.

HMS *Reward* leading drifters of the Dover Patrol in 1917. The drifters were mainly taken up from the fishing industry but many were built for the navy during the war too.

R.M.S. ARCADIAN

With a complement of 1,335 troops and crew, the Royal Mail Steam Packet Company's SS *Arcadian* had just performed a boat drill as the submarine UC74 sank her with a torpedo on 15 April 1917. 1,058 of the crew and soldiers were rescued but many were injured or killed when the ship sank in six minutes, some by timber sucked down as the ship sank and which was then shot back up, smashing bones and crushing the swimming men. In this view you can see the men hanging from ropes between the stern and the water.

MAY 1917

An all-too-familiar sight in 1917 as women and children wait in the bread queue. Although rationing itself wasn't introduced until early 1918, there were widespread shortages of flour and the King called upon the nation to eat less bread.

DOING THEIR BIT.

We Must All Eat Less Bread

On 2 May 1917, in a royal proclamation, the King called upon the nation to reduce the consumption of bread. The U-boat attacks on merchant shipping were causing shortages of food and the Ministry of Food was tasked with making the nation more self-sufficient. An additional 3 million acres of land were taken over for farming, much of it worked by the Women's Land Army. Despite these measures, basics such as flour, butter, eggs, milk and meat remained in short supply and the public was urged to avoid all waste, in particular to save bread as this was the staple diet of the poorer classes. Food rationing was not introduced until early 1918 and it did little to address the inequalites in food supply. For those with plenty, the cartoonists and poster writers had to spell it out. 'If you are rich, defeat for Great Britain is at your command,' stated a notice in one store. 'In honour bound, do you live within the national scale of rations.'

Wartime recipe books suggested a number of alternatives to traditional ingredients, such as the use of potatoes in place of flour, and their pages offered new culinary delights such as ox brain fritters, fish custard and trench pudding. In the words of one recipe book author, 'If you cannot have the best, make the best of what you have.'

Top of page: Punch cartoon, published in September 1917.

Above: A prisoner appears
before a Food Control Court.
These mock trials were intended
to teach schoolchildren the
importance of not wasting food.

Right: 'The Price of Victory', a
cartoon published in May 1917.
'Well, old girl, if we can't do that
much, we don't deserve to win.'

A French anti-aircraft gun team on the Salonika Front, also known as the Macedonia Front. By 1917 the Allied Army of the Orient – a unified multi-national force under the command of France's General Maurice Sarrial – had been reinforced with divisions from France, Serbia, Britain, Italy, Greece and Russia.

The Twelfth Battle of the Isonzo took place from 24 October to 19 November 1917, and was fought between the Italians and the Austro-Hungarian forces in an area that is mostly in present-day Slovenia. *Above:* An Italian anti-aircraft gun. *Below:* 265,000 Italians were taken prisoner. The Italians suffered heavy losses with around 10,000 killed.

Above: A ferry crossing on the Isonzo river.

Below: Projectiles for the 'bombarde'.

Left: Map showing the southern sector of the Isonzo valley.

Lawrence of Arabia

One of the most enigmatic of characters in the First World War was Thomas Edward Lawrence, an archaeologist who was an expert in Arab history and culture. Born illegitimately in Wales in August 1888, Lawrence was killed as the result of a motorbike crash in 1935 in Dorset. His war was recorded, though, by American journalist and film maker Lowell Thomas, who toured after the war with a film and talk of Lawrence's adventures. Lawrence himself wrote two epics about the Middle East: *Seven Pillars of Wisdom* and the abridged version covering *The Revolt in the Desert*. Both were huge sellers. David Lean's film entitled *Lawrence of Arabia* helped secure the everlasting fame of T. E. Lawrence.

Lawrence had been co-opted prior to the start of the war to help the British Army with a survey of the Negev desert under the pretext of archaeological excavations and when war started Lawrence was coopted into the army as an intelligence officer in Cairo in October 1914. He had spent time as an officer in the Oxford University OTC so was no stranger to army life.

At the start of the war, Lawrence had provided the British Army with a detailed map of the Negev desert's resources, including water supplies and other strategic targets. The Foreign Office's policy in the Middle East, which was primarily Ottoman controlled, was to provoke a campaign of internal insurgency. The Foreign Office had determined that the Arab tribes would support this, as long as they were financed and armed. The effort required by the Turks to contain this revolt would undermine their troops and resources

Lawrence of Arabia – T. E. Lawrence – in local dress.

elsewhere, helping the overall war effort. Basically, the cost of supporting a revolt would be cheap but the cost of fighting it would be enormous, thousands of times more costly in terms of men and resources than the cost of supporting a revolution.

Lawrence, with his intimate knowledge of the Levant and Syria, was sent by the Foreign Office to work with the Hashemite forces in the Hejaz in October 1916. He fought with the irregular troops of Emir Faisal, the son of Sharif Hussein of Mecca, in guerilla operations. With the assistance of the Royal Navy, in December 1916, he helped the Arabs turn back an attack by the Turks on Yanbu. Lawrence helped convince the Arabs to fight together in coordinated campaigns against the Turks. Instead of making a frontal assault on Turkish-held Medina, Lawrence encouraged the Arabs to leave the Turkish garrisons there and tie up huge numbers of troops while the Arabs attacked the Hejaz railway, which supplied the garrison. As a result, more Turkish troops were tied up protecting the railway and repairing the damage caused. Much British money and equipment was given to Emir Faisal to continue the fight.

In the spring of 1917, after an unsuccessful attack on Medina, the forces of the Arab Revolt seized the Red Sea ports of Yanbu and Wejh. A period of relative inaction as the British and Arabs decided on the next course of action saw the Arabs attack the Hejaz railway. The main British force was positioned opposite the Gaza–Beersheba line and Faisal proposed attacking Medina. Lawrence convinced Faisal to attack Aqaba, the Jordanian port on the Red Sea. Aqaba had been used by the Turks during their 1915 attack on the Suez Canal and the town threatened the British advance into Palestine. Holding the port also meant that the Arab Revolt could be supplied as it approached Palestine too. The British in Cairo expected Lawrence and the Arabs to fail so did not take the attack seriously. Lawrence arranged with the various northern Bedouin to support the revolt and they joined in the attack on Aqaba. Aqaba, at the time, was a small village and the nearest Turkish garrison was at Wadi Itm and was composed of only 300 soldiers. Attack from the sea was possible but difficult. Marines had landed there in 1916 and British ships had shelled the village but there was a lack of landing beaches and no real port. From the landward side, the impassable Nefud desert protected the village.

In May 1917, the Bedouins, with Lawrence, began to cross the desert. Lawrence had managed to make the leader of the northern Howeitat tribe, Auda Abu Tayi, join the revolt. Only the heat of the desert and attacks by snakes and scorpions caused the Arabs a problem and they reached the Wadi Sirhan area, and paid the Rualla Arabs £6,000 to let them use the area as a base. On the way, they destroyed sections of the Hejaz Railway. Lawrence planned to make the Turks think that Damascus was the target of the Arab Revolt and destroying a railway bridge at Baalbek and the capture of a railway station at Daraa persuaded the Turks that Damascus or Aleppo were the target. 400 Turkish cavalry were sent to chase the Arabs but the Arabs managed to escape the trap. The main battle for Aqaba took place on 2 July, not at the village

Above: T. E. Lawrence, suited this time, walking behind Winston Churchill at the Cairo Conference held in March 1921. This was convened to establish British policy for the Middle East, and Lawrence lobbied on behalf of Emir Faisal, the king of Syria and Iraq at that time.

itself, but at a Turkish blockhouse at Abu al Lasan, halfway between Aqaba and Ma'an. Some Arab rebels had captured the blockhouse a few days before but had been attacked and the Turks had regained the small fort. As retaliation, the Turks attacked a nearby Arab settlement, killing numerous Arabs. Auda led the attack personally and it was a great success. Many Turks were brutally killed by the Arabs before they could be restrained. Two Arabs died for 300 Turkish dead and 300 captured. Lawrence accidentally shot his camel but was thrown clear and survived this misfortune. Some British naval vessels arrived at Aqaba and began to shell the village and Lawrence, Auda and Nasir, with 5,000 Arabs, entered Aqaba, and the garrison surrendered to them.

Lawrence himself headed back for Cairo, crossing over the Sinai Peninsula, to inform Allenby that Aqaba had fallen once he had reached the Suez Canal. The navy sent supplies by sea. Within the next few days, more weapons and supplies were sent to Aqaba, along with numerous small warships. It would take all summer for Aqaba to be secured but the arrival of the navy warships and aircraft prevented the Turks from trying to attack and conquer Aqaba again. Faisal's army could now be transported north and begin to support the British again. The Turks in Medina were isolated and the way was open for Arab revolution in Syria and the rest of Jordan.

Lawrence had proven himself, both to Faisal and to General Allenby. He had united the disparate Arab tribes into a cohesive fighting force that would go on to conquer Damascus in October 1918. Lawrence tried, and failed, to convince his superiors of the need for a combined Arab state. The failure of the Allied powers to sort out the Middle East at the end of the First World War has ultimately led to the problems the region has today. Perhaps if T. E. Lawrence had been listened to, then the fate of Middle East politics may have been rather different. We shall never know, but the failure to provide support to the Arabs and to find a resolution to the challenges of the Jews in Palestine that accommodated the other religions in the area is a problem that 100 years later is still to be resolved.

Below: A patrol of the Imperial Camel Corps in Gaza in 1917.

Above: With the loss of the Furness Bermuda ships to the Navy for use as troopships, Bermuda itself still needed a passenger vessel for communication with the United States. The rather decrepit and old HMS *Charybdis* was converted for passenger service and for the duration served as Bermuda's lifeline with America. *Below:* The British minelayer *City of Paris* had been converted from the Ellerman Line's steamship. Keeping her name for naval service, this view was taken by the famous naval photographers Sadler & Renouf, who took many views of the surrendered German fleet at Scapa Flow.

In May 1917 General Philippe Pétain was appointed as Commander-in-Chief of the French Army, replacing General Nivelle whose failed Chemin des Dames offensive had provoked widespread mutinies within the army. (In the Second World War Pétain became Prime Minister of Vichy France, and after the war he was put on trial for treason.)

JUNE 1917

In 1917 the Zeppelin raiders were superceded by Germany's Gotha aircraft. In the event of a raid, police cars advised the inhabitants of London to take cover.

The Gotha raids. *Above:* Loading bombs on to a German Gotha aircraft. On 25 May and 5 June 1917 attempts were made to attack London, but the bombers were diverted by poor weather to other targets. Then, on 13 June, the first daylight raid on the capital resulted in 162 deaths, including sixteen children when a bomb fell on a school in Poplar. Londoners had not been prepared for daylight raids and many crowded into the street to watch. As the defences improved, the Gothas turned to night raids instead, with the first of these taking place in September – see page 78. *Below:* Cutaway of a Gotha bomber's fuselage.

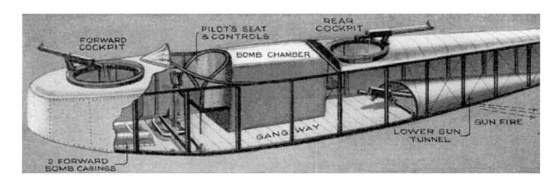

Above: A group of infants is lead to an air-raid shelter. 'On the whole the children behaved well throughout the war, and especially in the exciting time of air raids and the indiscriminate throwing of bombs by Zeppelins began, were very nervous, but this nervousness almost entirely passed...' Extract from *The Times History of the War*, published in 1918.

Right: These girls are taking part in an air-raid drill, practising carrying a wounded 'schoolfellow'.

Bomb damage at the base of Cleopatra's Needle on the Thames Embankment. This was caused on the first night raid by the Gothas on 4/5 September. As well as exposing the Underground beneath the Embankment, the bomb damaged a tram, killing two people, and left its mark on the base of the Sphinx.

Above: Royal Navy mobile anti-aircraft guns were used in the defence of London against the Gothas.
Below: London County Council ambulance girls provided a fast response for those injured in the air raids. Note the tin helmets normally worn by those fighting at the Front.

Above: A Women's Reserve Ambulance with members of the Green Cross Society. Women also served on the Home Front in the Women Police Volunteers. *Below:* Much was made of the deaths of children in air raids, as if British bombs were more discriminate. This image of two child victims at Ramsgate was published in *The Graphic* in 1917 under the headline, 'The massacre of the innocents by Herod, otherwise Wilhelm II, king of the Huns'.

Above: Ships were being sunk at such a rate that shipbuilding was finding it hard to keep up. Some ships did not last long. Elders & Fyffes' *Cavina* lasted from 1915 until 1 June 1917, when she was sunk by U88 some 45 miles off Fastnet en route from Limon to Avonmouth with a cargo of bananas and logwood. *Below:* HMS *Warspite*, firing a broadside of her 15-inch guns. She was oil-fired and her guns were a new size when first introduced. She survived both wars and was destroyed in Prussia Cove, Cornwall, while on the way to the breakers' yard.

Interned German ships
Very quickly, upon America's entry into the war, German ships interned in US ports were taken over by the US Navy and converted to troopships and used in the build-up of American troops in France. *Above:* Germany's four-funneled ships interned at Newport News and Hoboken were all commandered for this purpose.

Opposite page, top: Two German ships, the one behind a four-stacker already painted in grey. *Opposite, bottom:* The USS *Mount Vernon*, the ex-*Kronprinzessin Cecile*, captured in Bar Harbor, Maine, in 1914, is used as a troopship taking US soldiers to France in 1917.

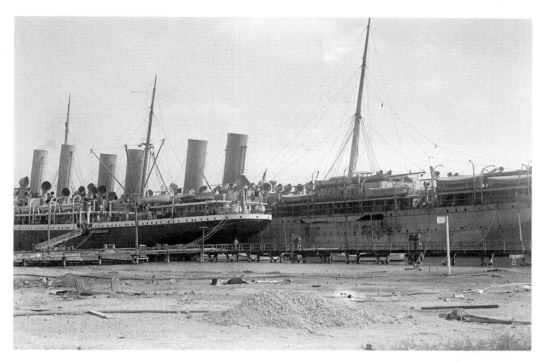

American troop convoy to France.

Troop convoys

The US troop convoys were dispatched from the eastern seaboard of the USA to Brest and St Nazaire, France. *Above:* A convoy of passenger liners, all painted in a dazzle-paint scheme. Dazzle paint was intended to confuse rather than camouflage and the abstract paint designs were intended to make it difficult for the submarines to work out in which direction a ship was travelling. Other ships, below, were painted in an all-over battleship grey.

13426

Some of the 300,000 Americans a month that were arriving by early 1918. They would change the course of the war in the Allies' favour very quickly.

Above: American troops disembark at Brest. Almost none of the Americans that arrived in Europe in 1918 travelled via the UK. All were shipped to western French ports. *Below:* Marines being taken by train to camps close to the front line.

Above: Newly arrived American marines digging trenches in France. *Below:* A highly staged photograph of the Americans 'in action' during a gas attack. As you can see, only five of the six soldiers are wearing gasmasks and one man has not got his mask on in time.

Above: USS *Massachusetts* was used for target practice during the First World War, being commissioned in 1917 to train gun crews. She was scuttled in 1921 off Florida and used as a target for gunnery practice. She is now an artificial reef. *Below:* USS *Oregon* was used to take US troops to Russia in the latter stages of the war. After the war ended, she was preserved in Portland, Oregon, but cannibalised for her metal during the Second World War. She was finally scrapped in 1956 in Japan.

Above: Launched in 1904, the cruiser USS *San Diego* was built as the USS *California* originally. She was used in 1918 to protect convoys to Europe, sailing out of Nova Scotia and Portsmouth, New Hampshire. On 19 July 1918, an explosion damaged her below the waterline and she began to sink, being the only major ship lost by the US Navy during the war. Six died in the tragedy. It was assumed that a German mine was to blame for the explosion.

Right: Inside the engine room of a US battleship.

S.S. Illinois sinking with German sub in foreground.

Above: The SS *Illinois* was one of three US merchant ships sunk in a single day in March 1917. Despite showing an American flag on her stern and painted on her flanks, a German U-boat dispatched her to the bottom. It was the sinking of these vessels that effectively made Congress agree to go to war. *Below:* US submarines in dry dock. Having more naval ships available due to the entry of the USA into the war helped change the balance of the war almost immediately.

Above: Wreck of Tribal class destroyer HMS *Nubian* at Foreland, near Folkestone, Kent. She was wrecked on 26 October 1916 and was part salvaged. Her stern was recovered and the bow section of HMS *Zulu*, which had hit a mine on 8 November 1916, was also recovered and the two parts stitched together to make HMS *Zubian*. The *Zubian* was commissioned on 7 June 1917 and scrapped in 1919. *Below:* The armed merchant cruiser HMS *Patia* had once transported bananas for Elders & Fyffes but the war years were spent as an AMC. She is shown here off Dakar in 1917 but she was sunk by UC-49 on 13 June 1918 in the Bristol Channel. Sixteen died in the sinking.

A GOOD RIDDANCE.

[The KING has done a popular act in abolishing the German titles held by members of His Majesty's family.]

It wasn't until 1917 that the pressure of anti-German feelings persuaded the King to sweep away the ties with his German cousins. All German titles were relinquished and the House of Saxe-Coburg-Gotha became the more British-sounding House of Windsor. This *Punch* cartoon was published in June 1917.

JULY 1917

A rescue station in an Australian tunnelling system. The soldier is wearing breathing apparatus and he also carries a canary in a cage to detect the presence of poisonous gas.

HMS *Cossack* was damaged by one of her own depth charges on 1 July 1917. She had collided with the transport *The Duchess* off Eastbourne and some of her depth charges were dropped, damaging her. She was towed to dry dock and repaired.

On 4 July 1917, the minesweeping sloop HMS *Azalea*, shown above, hit a mine and was badly damaged. She was salvaged and scrapped in 1923.

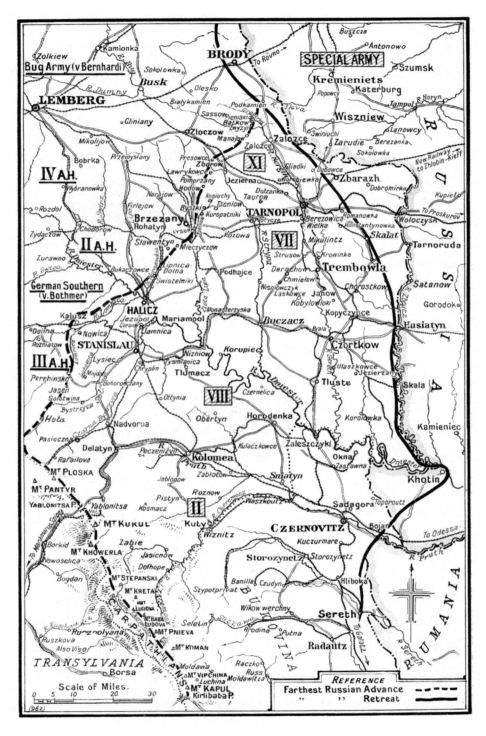

Area of the Russian retreat, showing the positions of the respective armies, July 1917.

Above: According to the original caption on this photograph, this is said to be a 'German officer disguised as an Austrian blind beggar, with a pretended wife and child.' In truth this appears to be pure invention by the propagandists.

Left: Men of the Polish Legion in the Russian army.

Austrian poster for war savings bonds featuring an infantryman holding a stick-grenade.

AMERICA'S COMMANDER-IN-CHIEF

General John J. Pershing landed in England on June 8, 1917, and proceeded to France on June 13. It was not till a year later, however, that he led American troops to their first notable victory in the Saint Mihiel salient. He is here seen disembarking at Boulogne

Above: American troops first
appeared in London on
14 August 1917. They are seen
here marching along Piccadilly on
their way to Buckingham Palace,
where they were to be inspected
by the king.

Right: 'First in France' – poster
featuring the US Marines.

Opposite page: The US
Commander-in-Chief, General
Pershing, landed in England on
8 June and continued on to
France five days later. He is shown
disembarking at Boulogne.

When the USA eneterd the war they not only brought with them their enormous industrial might and manpower, but also a new approach to the war poster. The three posters featuring tanks, shown above and opposite, feature strong, vivid colours. 'Hero Land' and 'Over There' are not war posters as such, as they promote movies featuring the tanks.

Left: A far more muted palette for this poster appealing for drivers to join the American Field Service.

SEE REAL WARFARE
"OVER THERE" CANTONMENT
MADE POSSIBLE BY BLOOD—NOT MONEY

5TH REGIMENT ARMORY
BALTIMORE

OPENS
MARCH 30TH

Moving Pictures
Music
Worlds greatest
Orators

TICKETS FOR SALE HERE

Lloyd Harrison

H. GAMSE & BRO. LITHO. BALTO. MD.

JOURNÉE DE L'ARMÉE D'AFRIQUE
ET DES TROUPES COLONIALES

DEVAMBEZ, PARIS

ARMIA POLSKA WE FRANCYI
POLISH ARMY IN FRANCE
CENTRUM REKRUTACYJNE №.
RECRUITING CENTRE

W.T. BENDA

The Americans and Commonwealth countries were not the only ones to send men to fight for the Allies. *Opposite page:* The French had their own empire and this poster shows troops from the African colonies. *Above:* A very dramatic portrayal of a Polish soldier fighting in France.

Pegasus at Work for the Allies

American Poets' Ambulances in Italy, 1917

America's participation also spilled over into the work of the charitable and fund-raising organisations involved in providing for the servicemen and the populations of the occupied countries.

Above: American Poets' Ambulances in Italy, 1917. 'In honour of the victims of the *Lusitania.*'

Left: American Fund for the French Wounded, printed in France and showing the Paris Depot.

Above: The American Committee for Devastated Regions of France.

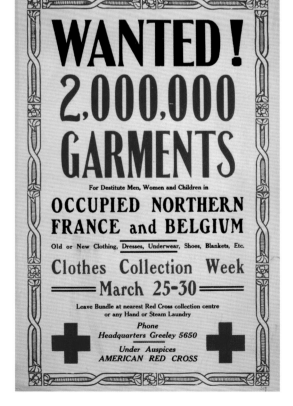

Left: Appeal for 2 million garments for the destitute men, women and children in occupied Northern France and Belgium.

THE AIR RAIDER

'it er 'Arry!'

K BAUER

By 1917 the Zeppelin raiders were taking a beating from the strengthened anti-aircraft defences and improvements in the performance of fighter aircraft.
Above: A typical postcard from the period.
Above right: Ferdinand Graf von Zeppelin, the retired cavalry officer and father of the Zeppelin airships, died on 8 March 1917, aged seventy-eight.

Right: Poster for the US Air Service, which began operations in France as the US Army Air Service in the spring of 1918.

Opposite page: British SE5, shown top, and the Red Baron's Flying Circus bringing down a British fighter in a dog fight, bottom. It is a myth that all of of Manfred von Richthofen's aircraft were painted entirely in red. However, this illustration does depict the iconic Dr.1 triplane in its bright scarlet colours.

JOIN THE
AIR SERVICE
and
SERVE
in
FRANCE

DO IT
NOW

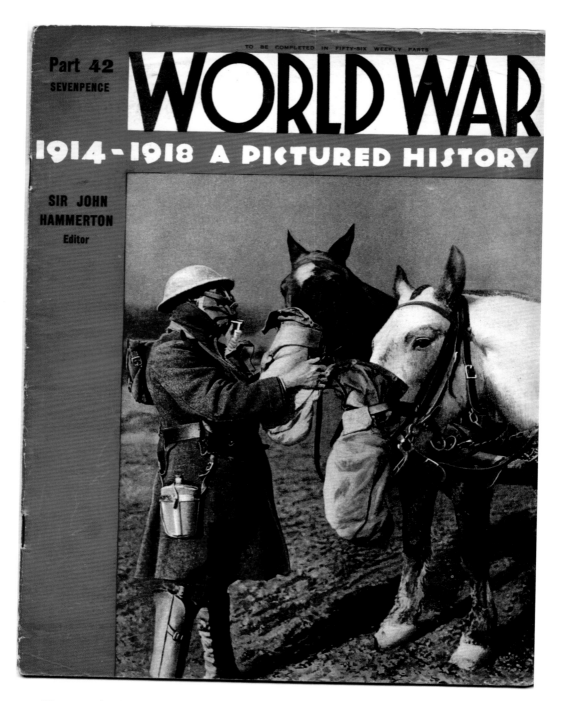

Part 42
SEVENPENCE

WORLD WAR

1914-1918 A PICTURED HISTORY

SIR JOHN HAMMERTON
Editor

There was hardly a family in Britain that hadn't been affected by the war, and this accounted for an appetite for accounts of the war, such as this partwork, above. The cover image shows horses being fitted with masks to protect against a gas attack.

Above: Men of the Leicestershire Regiment, known as the Tigers, enjoy a respite from the fighting, sharing a captured trench near Ribecourt with machine-gunners on 20 November 1917.

Right: A more cosy portrayal of life for the Tommies in the trenches. The Church Army and the YMCA both provided huts where the men from the front could rest.

Wetherby Flag Day

THURSDAY, 29th MARCH, 1917.

PLEASE HELP US TO GIVE THESE REAL NECESSITIES.

"YOU'LL FIND ALL YOU WANT"
IN A **HUT** OF THE
CHURCH ARMY

**800 ALREADY ERECTED ON ALL BRITISH FIGHTING FRONTS.
120 ADDITIONAL HUTS NEEDED FOR WESTERN FRONT.**

Sketched on spot by Y.M.C.A. secy   Coquemer imp. paris.

VERDUN
ROAD TO Y.M.C.A. CANTEEN

Opposite page, and right, top and middle: Posters for the YMCA showing a dugout in France and a hut at a London railway station. The YMCA supported the fighting men through a range of services, including entertainment and recreational activities, rest programmes for the battle-weary, and leave centres. These included 4,000 huts and some 1,500 canteens.

A Y.M.C.A. "DUG-OUT" IN FRANCE.

Y.M.C.A. 3 A.M. IN A LONDON STATION HUT Y.M.C.A.

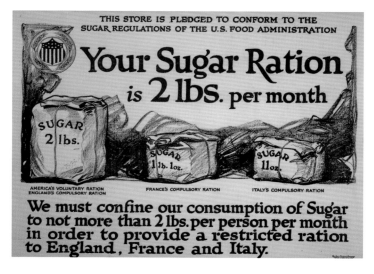

THIS STORE IS PLEDGED TO CONFORM TO THE SUGAR REGULATIONS OF THE U.S. FOOD ADMINISTRATION

Your Sugar Ration *is* 2 lbs. per month

SUGAR 2 lbs.

SUGAR 1 lb. 1oz.

SUGAR 11oz.

AMERICA'S VOLUNTARY RATION ENGLAND'S COMPULSORY RATION

FRANCE'S COMPULSORY RATION

ITALY'S COMPULSORY RATION

We must confine our consumption of Sugar to not more than 2 lbs. per person per month in order to provide a restricted ration to England, France and Italy.

Right: The American public were not unaffected by the war in Europe and, as this poster shows, some commodities were rationed there too.

The winter of 1917/18 led to a comparative lull in the activity of both sides between Cambrai and the March offensive of 1918. The conditions made movement difficult and treacherous as shell craters and other obstacles were hidden under the blanket of snow.

During the Russian offensive of July 1917, the second wave await the order to advance. This Siberian force captured Dzike-Lany, a fortified summit south-west of Brzezany.

Above: Just before midnight on 9 July 1917, cordite exploded aboard HMS *Vanguard* while she lay at anchor at Scapa Flow. The St Vincent class ship was built at Barrow-in-Furness and commissioned in 1910. 804 out of 806 aboard died when she exploded and the disaster remains the biggest loss of life from an accidental explosion in the United Kingdom.

The sinking of HMS *Vanguard*

HMS *Vanguard* was torn apart by an explosion while at anchor in Scapa. She had been laid down on 2 April 1908 and launched on 22 February 1909 at the Barrow-in-Furness yard of Armstrong Vickers. She had been built during the naval arms race that ultimately led to the First World War and was allocated to the First Battle Fleet at the start of the war and based at Scapa Flow. Along with twenty-three other Dreadnoughts, she saw action at Jutland but left the battle unscathed.

She would succumb not to a German shell or mine but to an internal explosion while at Scapa on 9 July 1917. Just before midnight, surrounded by other ships of the fleet, she was wrecked by a huge explosion, which tore her apart.

Commissioned on 1 March 1910, *Vanguard* was a St Vincent-class Dreadnought, displacing 19,560 tons and being 500 feet in length. She was powered by four Parsons turbines and was capable of 21.7 knots, with a range of 6,900 miles. She had ten 12-inch guns in five turrets, and twelve 4-inch guns, as well as three torpedo tubes.

Apart from firing at an unknown target on 1 September 1914, and from her time at the Battle of Jutland, *Vanguard* led a rather uneventful war until 9 July 1917. That day her crew had spent the afternoon practicing drill, including abandoning ship. At 6.30 p.m. *Vanguard* anchored at the northern end of Scapa Flow and her crew settled down for their evening routine. No one on *Vanguard* or the other ships of the fleet noticed anything amiss until the sky was lit by a huge explosion at 11.20 p.m. Soon, chunks of *Vanguard* were raining down on other nearby vessels, with the largest section being a 5-foot-by-6-foot piece which landed on the deck of HMS *Bellerophon*. This part had come from the central dynamo room.

A subsequent Court of Enquiry was held and called many witnesses from nearby vessels. It was concluded that a small explosion had been seen between the foremast and A turret, followed by two much larger explosions. On the balance of evidence either Magazine P or Q, or indeed both, had exploded, probably caused by the cordite overheating and spontaneously combusting. In all, 804 men died, with just two survivors. *Vanguard* lies in Scapa Flow as a memorial to one of the worst disasters in British naval history, made all the worse by probably being preventable. Many of her crew are buried in a mass grave near to where their ship was destroyed.

A dummy battleship! The Shire Line's SS *Perthshire* in disguise as HMS *Vanguard*. From a distance, the disguise would fool the Germans but up close the ships did not look similar.

Femme fatale Mata Hari was an exotic dancer who was accused of being a double agent, using her powers of seduction to extract secrets from her lovers which she passed on to the Germans. Arrested in Paris in August, she was convicted of spying, despite a lack of any hard evidence, and executed by firing squad on 15 October 1917.

AUGUST 1917

American soldiers practice repairing phone lines during a simulated gas attack.

On 14 August 1917 the Chinese abandoned their stance of neutrality and declared war on Germany. *Above:* Sun Yat-Sen on the way to the tomb of the first Ming Emperor. *Below:* Chinese officers studying European warfare methods and tactics with the French army in 1917.

Above: On 2 August Squadron Commander H. Dunning made the first landing on a ship under way when he put his Sopwith Pup down on the deck of the carrier HMS *Furious*. In a strong headwind, the biplane appears to be almost hovering above the deck. *Below:* Photograph of an Italian seaplane published in *Il Mondono* in February 1917.

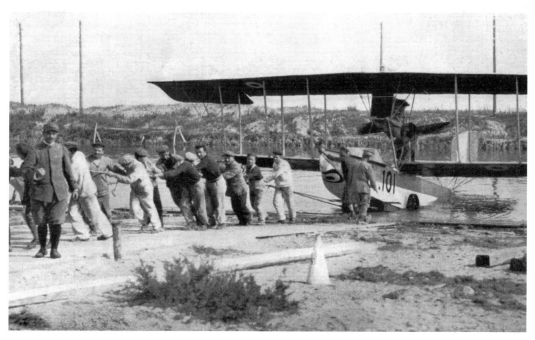

Above: Allied observation balloons were used at Ypres to spot for the artillery and to observe the enemy's movements on the ground.

The Muddy Third Battle of Ypres

Primarily a British and Commonwealth battle, the Third Battle of Ypres, or Passchendaele, took place between July and November 1917. It was fought over the ridges south and east of Ypres, Belgium, and was part of a wider campaign to attack to the north and open up the occupied land along Belgium's coast. A large railway junction lay at Roeselare and this was an important part of the supply route for the German troops. Passchendaele was a mere 5 miles from this important junction. The next target after this was an advance to Torhout, thereby closing the German railway line to Roeselare. For the Allies, the determination of the German Fourth Army, the weather and a terrifying bombardment that had destroyed the natural drainage and turned the shell-cratered land into mud destroyed any hope of the plan succeeding in its entirety. Britain and France both had to send troops and weapons to Italy to bolster the Italians after their failed offensives along the Isonzo river. The battle only ended after four and a half months when Canadian troops finally managed to capture Passchendaele.

A campaign in Flanders was controversial in 1917 and has remained so. British Prime Minister Lloyd George opposed the offensive, as did General Foch, the French

Chief of the General Staff. The British commander Field Marshal Sir Douglas Haig did not receive approval for the Flanders operation from the War Cabinet until 25 July. Matters of dispute among the participants and writers and historians since the war have included the wisdom of pursuing an offensive strategy in the wake of the failed Nivelle Offensive, rather than waiting for the arrival of the American armies in France; the choice of Flanders over areas further south or the Italian front; the climate and weather in Flanders; Haig's selection of General Hubert Gough and the Fifth Army to conduct the offensive; debates over the nature of the opening attack between advocates of shallow and deeper objectives; the passage of time between the Battle of Messines and the opening attack of the Battles of Ypres; the extent to which the internal troubles of the French armies motivated British persistence in the offensive; the effect of mud on operations; the decision to continue the offensive in October once the weather had broken; and the human

Below: One of the most iconic scenes of the entire war, showing soldiers trudging through the muddy and blasted remains of what had once been the Chateau Wood in Ypres.

Above: Australian troops come together for a briefing, Ypres, October 1917. *Below:* Dugout headquarters near Hooge Crater during the Third Battle of Ypres. The crater, beside the Menin Road, had been created by the detonation of a massive British mine the previous year.

cost of the campaign on the soldiers of the German and British armies. During the battle, the French army suffered a series of mutinies that saw the British and their Commonwealth allies shore up the French defence.

The planning for the offensive had begun months in advance, with the doubling of the railway lines close to the front, as well as the moving of hundreds of thousands of shells and millions of rounds of ammunition. The plan at Passchendaele was for a battle of attrition. It was an area the Germans could not afford to lose and any battle would weaken their forces. The added impetus of America entering the war only helped this simple war of numbers.

The initial stage was to attack the Messines ridge. Looking down onto Ypres, these positions dominated the battlefield and needed to be taken. Since 1915, the British had been mining underneath the battlefield and twenty-one mines had been dug and loaded with 450 tons of explosives. On 7 June 1917, they were set off, with two failing to detonate. The other nineteen were set off at 0310. The shock of the mines was so great that British casualties on that first day were light, even though the British had expected 50 per cent casualties. Until 14 June, the fighting continued on the east of the ridge but the Germans had pretty much been cleared off the ridge by then.

The battle kept the Germans from sending too many troops to attack the Russians, who opened the Kerensky offensive on 1 July too. The Russian morale was lacking and they were soon in retreat but the diversion of German forces in both Flanders and the East kept the Germans from really making huge gains in their counter-attacks.

The main battle began on 31 July, with the objectives being the German Wilhelm Line, its third line of defence. At 0350 the attack began; it had most success to the north. Here, the Allied forces captured and advanced over some 3,000 yards of ground. In the centre of the attack an advance of 4,000 yards was made but the Germans counter-attacked the flanks and pushed back the British troops with 70 per cent casualties. Late in the day, mud, artillery and machine-gun fire stopped the counter-attack.

On 10 August, an attempt was made to capture the land lost on 31 July. German artillery and machine-gun fire as well as counter-attacks saw British infantry trapped in Glencorse wood. A German infantry division attacked at 1900 and managed to recapture all but the north-east sector of the wood. Casualties overall were around half of those made during the attack on the Somme the previous year.

Between 15 and 25 August, the Canadian Corps and five divisions of German troops fought it out near Lens with the Germans defeated and the reserve armies that could have made a difference at Passchendaele 'fought out'. The Battle of Langemarck took place between 16 and 18 August. In a re-run of the battle around Glencorse wood, the Germans counter-attacked and forced the British back to the start line. British artillery forced the Germans back a little, having inflicted huge casualties in the counter-attack. Further north, XVIII Corps took and held St Julien and the area south of Langemarck. Langemarck was captured and the French First

Above: Scottish troops laying barbed wire entanglements. Developed in the USA to restrain cattle, barbed wire was used extensively by all sides throughout the war.

Army took the Kortebeek river and St Jansbeck stream. Heavy casualties occurred due to German artillery firing on the new lines beyond Langemarck. On 20 August, British soldiers captured areas around the St Julien road and more land was taken two days later, still, unfortunately, under the cover of German guns. Attempts between 22 and 24 August to capture Glencorse wood saw huge casualties on both sides. The weather turned at the end of the month and heavy rain fell, turning the land into mud.

The weather prevented both sides from fighting properly and to the best of their abilities. The German counter-attacks had seen much of the land lost regained but the Allies changed the commander of the battle to General Plumer, who intended to fight the battle in small chunks, taking time to take each ridge and consolidate each win before undertaking the next. The series of fights that took place saw the German troops ground down, with little opportunity for rest and recuperation. On 20 September, the British attacked again, with objectives of around a mile. A few hours after dawn, the day's objectives were reached and the Germans too slow to bring their reserves to play. Having to cross almost two miles of mud had slowed them down, giving the British time to bed down. After defeats on 26 September, the Germans changed their tactics. They had had to, not expecting the cautious approach taken by the Allies. The improvements in the weather had meant the

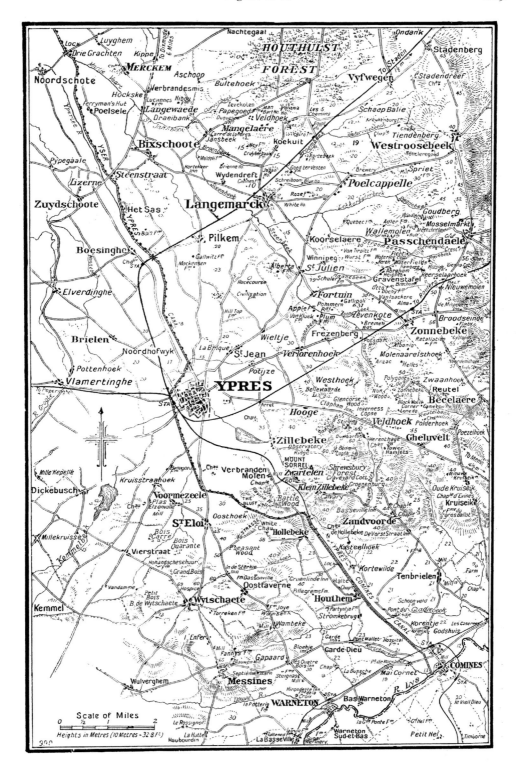

Above: Materials for creating the entanglements have been brought up during the Battle of Menin Heights. *Below:* German officers captured by the Canadians on Hill 70. This had been a localised action intended to draw German forces away from the main battle at Ypres.

British could bring up more artillery shells and the defence they could muster by the time the Germans counter-attacked meant serious defeats for the Germans. The Germans brought all their machine guns forward, even those in reserve, and reinforced the front lines with reserves. Attempts to bring the German artillery to bear and to encourage the British to bring more troops to the front were thwarted. Some twenty-four attacks were made between 26 September and 3 October, all ending in failure for the Germans. A full-scale German counter-attack was planned for 4 October.

Various battles took place in September, including the Battle for Menin Road Bridge between 20 and 25 September and the Battle of Polygon Wood between 26 September and 3 October. On 4 October, the Battle of Brooseinde took place. It was the last battle before the rains returned and the Germans counter-attacked but their losses were terribly high.

On 9 October, the Battle of Poelcappelle took place but most of the captured ground could not be held due to the mud and German counter-attacks. On 12 October, the First Battle of Passchendaele took place. The troops on both sides were eaxhausted and the battle was inconclusive. 13,000 Allied casualties included 2,375 New Zealanders, of whom 845 were dead or wounded and stranded in

Australian troops near Idiots Corner during the Third Battle of Ypres.

no man's land. The next day, the attacks were called off until the weather improved. On 23 October, the Battle of Malmaison took place, when the French attacked, taking pressure off the Ypres front. The Germans were swiftly defeated and 11,157 prisoners were taken by the French between then and 2 November. Minor operations on 20–22 October preceded the rather more major Second Battle of Passchendaele, which started on 26 October. With objectives reached, the next stage began on 30 October, with the ground prepared to capture Passchendaele. On 6 November, after three rainless days, the next stage of the battle began. The village was captured that day and the next four days saw the Canadians mopping up the remaining German defences to the north of the village.

The battles of that summer and autumn had worn the Germans down and it was a fight they would not fully recover from. The forthcoming battles would not be as muddy or as exhausting but the focus of battle would shift from Flanders further south. Campaigning in the north was almost over for the winter. British casualties were close to 250,000 but the Germans had lost 400,000, on top of which they also lost many more during the campaign in the East against the Russians. It was the beginning of the end for the Germans, who would soon face hundreds of thousands of Americans, with their almost unlimited weapons and supplies.

Above: HMS *Valiant* in dry dock. On 24 August 1916, she was damaged in collision with HMS *Warspite* and is shown here under repair. She managed to escape unscathed at Jutland and one of her 15-inch guns was used in the battery at Johore in the interwar years. *Below:* A rare postcard view showing the selling of a dead seaman's effects. Photographed aboard HMS *Valiant*, the sailors would buy the effects and the money would be sent to the widow.

Taken up while being built, the Great Eastern Railway steamer *Stockholm* was converted into the aircraft carrier HMS *Pegasus* and is shown here in Malta in August 1917. In 1919, she was used in the White Russian campaign in Archangel.

The Russian campaign on the Eastern Front took a new turn when the Bolsheviks overthrew the Russian Tzar. In late 1917, HMS *Caradoc* was in the Crimea, shelling the Bolsheviks. She ran aground off Fair Isle on 15 August 1917 but was salvaged and returned to service very quickly.

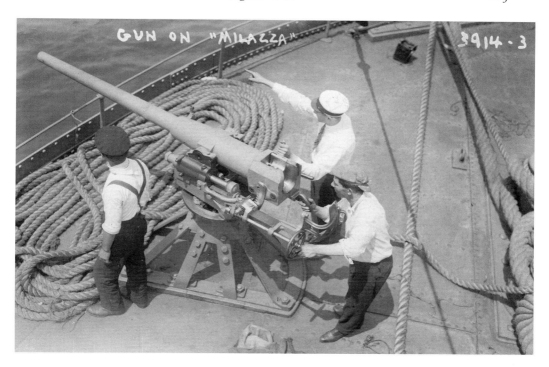

Above: The Italian vessel *Milazza* was the largest cargo ship in the world when she entered service in 1916. On 29 August 1917, she was sunk by an Austro-Hungarian U-boat. The U-14 was commanded by Georg Ritter von Trapp, who had married the granddaughter of the inventor of the torpedo, but von Trapp is more famous as the father in *The Sound of Music*.

We are familiar with the part played in the First World War by horses through Michael Morpurgo's *War Horse*, and also the birds that carried messages, but far less practical, at least for the most part, were the many animals kept as mascots or pets. Many ships had their cats or dogs, of course, but there were also pets among the infantry regiments at the Front. This selection of photographs was originally published in *The Graphic* in 1917. *Above:* Not really pets, these chickens ensured that the officers in the Dardenelles got their fresh eggs. *Below, from the left:* Leo the Great Dane belonged to the 2/6 North Staffordshires, and Biddy, the pet of HMS *Landrail,* saw action in both the Heligoland and Dogger Bank engagements. On the far right is an unidentified mule who was a mascot of the Royal Naval Division. Other notable pets and mascots included birds, goats and even the odd pig. See also, page 134.

SEPTEMBER 1917

Named after the famous Battle of Ramillies, HMS *Ramillies* was commissioned on 1 September 1917 after being built by Beardmore's at Dalmuir. Of 28,000 tons' displacement, she was 624 feet long and was armed with eight 15-inch guns. During her launch, her rudder was damaged and this meant she had to be towed to Cammell Laird's to go into dry dock and be repaired.

Above: A mobile water filter used by the British Army in France.

Trench Life – Of Lice and Men

In addition to coping with the daily dangers of enemy shells, snipers and the risk of gas attacks, the soldiers at the Front had to live in their trenches around the clock and in all weathers. The trenches stretched for 400 miles, going all the way from the North Sea down to the Swiss border. The way they were constructed depended on the widely varying ground conditions: chalky soil in the Somme area for example, or the mud of Ypres. At many times of the year the bottom of the trenches were under standing water and as a result many men suffered from a condition known as 'trench foot'. There were many other health hazards including poor sanitation and an infestation of rats and lice. The human lice, hair and body varieties, were a constant nuisance and it is said that no man living in the trenches could escape infestation. Rats, through their fleas, gnats and lice could spread diseases in addition to the discomfort that they caused. Measures were taken to kill and remove the rats, and when conditions allowed the bedlinen and soldiers' clothing would be washed and disinfected. Trench fever, also known as 'five day fever', was caused by the bacterium *Bartonella quintana*, which was transmitted by body lice. Symptons included a high fever, severe headaches, soreness of the eyes as well as the muscles in the legs and back, and pains in the shins.

Of all the parasites that infested the trenches, lice were the most prevalent and it became impossible to avoid becoming infested. *Above:* Human body lice, with the male on the left and the female on the right. *Below:* A special tank used to take infested bedclothes to the disinfecting chamber.

Above: A pyre for burning the clothes of the enemy dead. This was done to prevent the possibility of spreading infection.

Left: A portable disinfestor for treating bedclothes or clothing.

Above: Thousands of clean shirts for the British soldiers, hanging out to dry in the sunshine. *Below:* An Australian soldier is shown receiving his issue of clean underwear after a bath.

Daily life in the trenches could be extremely monotonous, with the time marked out by the daily chores or mealtimes, as shown above.

Left: An unexpected scene of contemplative study in the trenches. This is a cover illustration from the *Literary Digest*, published in October 1917, showing troops passing the time by studying French under the guidance of a French soldier.

Opposite page: Captain Bruce Bairnsfather's cartoons, featured in *Fragments From France*, portrayed the comical side of life in the trenches. They were hugely popular among the troops and ran to several volumes.

STILL MORE BYSTANDER FRAGMENTS *from* FRANCE

No.3

"Lets 'ave this pin of yours a minute I'll soon 'ave these winkles out of 'ere"

By Capt. Bruce Bairnsfather. 1/- NET

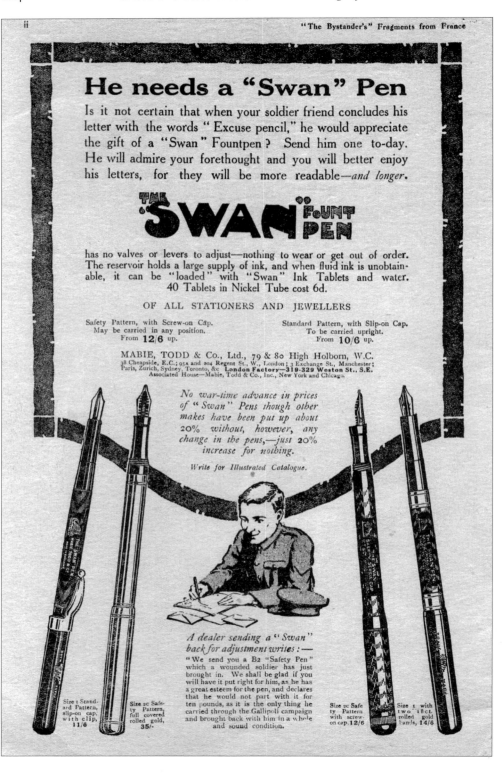

OCTOBER 1917

Above: The largest ship of the Russian Gulf of Riga Squadron, the pre-Dreadnought *Slava* was launched on 29 August 1903 and commissioned in October 1905. On 17 October 1917, *Slava* was involved in the Battle of Moon Sound and she was badly damaged by SMS *Koenig*. She was scuttled as a result near the island of Muhu. She was finally scrapped in 1935.

Opposite page: Back in Blighty the advertisers presented a somewhat anodyne version of trench life. At the bottom is an endorsement from a dealer who has sent a pen back for adjustment. 'We send you a B2 Safety Pen which a wounded soldier has just brought in. We shall be glad if you will have it put right for him, as he has a great esteem for the pen, and declares that he would not part with it for ten pounds, as it is the only thing he carried through the Gallipoli campaign and brought back with him in a whole and sound condition.'

Above: The L49 came down in woods near Bourbonne les Baines on 20 October 1917. The crew failed to destroy the ship and it remained intact for the Allies to examine in detail.

The Fall of the Zeppelin L49

As the war continued the Zeppelins were pushed to ever higher altitudes to escape their attackers, and to achieve this they underwent enormous technological advances. From the first military Zeppelins, the L3 class of 793,518 cubic feet, they grew to the six-engined L30 class or Type-R 'super Zepps' of 2,000,000 cubic feet and up to the ultimate L70 class Type-X of 2,196,300 cubic feet which, in the case of L71, had a theoretical range of around 7,460 miles and a ceiling of 20,000 feet. For the Allies the capture of German airships, in particular the L33, brought down near the village of Little Wigborough, Essex, in 1916, and the L49, which was forced down by French fighter aircraft near Bourbonne Les Baines and survived virtually intact in 1917, provided invaluable information for their own rigid airship designs. The Americans' ZR-1, the *Shenandoah*, was to be a virtual copy of the L49 while the L33 significantly influenced the design of the British R33 class, which included the R34, the first airship to cross the Atlantic (in 1919).

Two more views of the L49, including the interior, top. Although no longer airworthy it was in a good enough condition to provide the Allies with details of every aspect of its construction.

The October Rising in Russia, officially known as the Great October Socialist Revolution, was an armed insurrection led by the Bolsheviks in Petrograd on 7–8 November (24–25 October by the old calendar). Government buildings and the Winter Palace, the seat of the Provisional Government, were taken over.

Left: A cartoon by John McCutcheon showing Trotsky embracing the figure of Russia.

Below left: Vladimir Ilyich Lenin had returned to Petrograd in 1917, and in November that year he became the leader of the Russian Soviet Federative Socialist Republic.

Below right: The Marxist Leon Trotsky had joined the Bolsheviks shortly before the October Revolution and was elected chairman of the Petrograd Soviet.

Above: The trial of General Sukhomlinov in August/September 1917. The ex-Minister of War had been ousted from office amid allegations that he had failed to prepare the army and provide adequate armaments for the Great War. At the trial he was aquitted of a charge of treason, but found guilty of an abuse of power. In the event he served less than a year in prison. *Below:* A mass grave for the burial of the victims of the revolution in Petrograd.

Children march in Petrograd in a demonstration calling for the education of the people. After the revolution the ordinary people had a voice and the vast majority spoke through the party organisations calling for Russia's involvement in the war to be brought to an end.

Above: A Leninite demonstration in the Winter Palace Square in Petrograd. *Below:* The cruiser *Avrora* on the Neva at Petrograd, with her guns trained on the Winter Palace.

Above: HMS *Ivy*, an Anchusa class sloop, was built in 1917. She was sold in 1921. One of a class of twenty-eight, she was launched in October 1917 at Blyth. The sloops were designed for convoy duty.

Opposite page: Commissioned into the German Imperial Navy in 1916, SMS *Bremse* was a minelaying cruiser. In October 1917, she and her sister, *Brummer*, found a British convoy, sinking both destroyer escorts and nine of the twelve merchant ships. SMS *Bremse* survived the war but was sunk at Scapa Flow in 1919. In the world's greatest salvage effort, she was brought to the surface once more and scrapped.

SALVING GERMAN BATTLE-CRUISER, BREMSE, SCAPA FLOW.

BEEF.BLOCK

Pets were common aboard ship on most vessels from the smallest torpedo destroyer to the largest battleship. From the rather obvious cats and dogs to turtles, baby crocodiles, bears, tigers, donkeys, goats, antelopes and even a bat (HMS *Bat*'s mascot, of course), the pets were well loved by their crews, who buried them at sea if they died, and on land, in special graveyards, when close to their bases.

Beef Block, left, was a pet on HMS *Windsor*, while Side Boy, below, served on HMS *Neptune*.

See also, page 116.

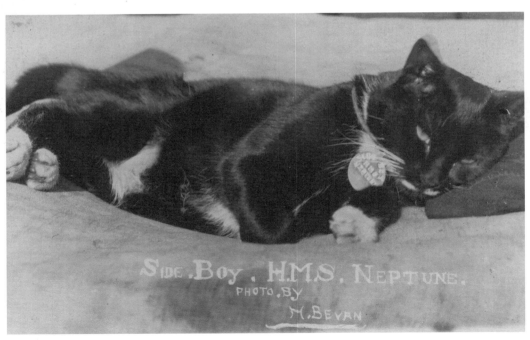

SIDE.BOY. HMS. NEPTUNE.
PHOTO.BY
M.BEVAN

NOVEMBER 1917

MYSTERY SHIP H M S HYDERABAD   4 INCH GUN MASKED   No 6.

The 4-inch gun of HMS *Hyderabad* disguised to look like a crate. She is shown here photographed in Liverpool in 1917. *Hyderabad* was one of the few specially built Q-ships, most being converted from merchant vessels. The Q-ships would patrol the sea lanes, awaiting attack from a U-boat. Often the U-boats would surface to shell the cargo vessel, which would then unmask its guns and shoot the submarine.

Cambrai

On the morning of 20 November 1917, the British Third Army, under General Sir Julian Byng, led the attack in what became known as the Battle of Cambrai. Although tanks had been introduced in 1916, Cambrai is recognised as the first major deployment of them in unprecedented numbers, with some 476 used by the British in a co-ordinated joint assault with artillery and infantry units. The plan was to take the Germans by surprise and punch a hole in the Hindenburg Line between the Canal de l'Escaut and the Canal du Nord, and to capture the Bourlon Ridge. The battle opened with a brief but intensive barrage by 1,000 guns. The first attacks, spearheaded by the Mark IV tanks, were hugely successful, and the Hindenburg Line was breached to a depth of 8 miles in parts. Only at Flesquières was the advance halted as the Germans knocked out many of the tanks, with the British co-ordination between infantry and tanks proving to be woefully lacking.

Despite initial successes, momentum was hard to maintain and the advance became bogged down as tanks succumbed to German artillery fire or suffered mechanical breakdowns. Although many of the tanks carried fascines – bundles of brushwood carried on the roof of a tank and used to fill trenches or gaps to enable them to pass over – the tanks became stuck and were picked off by the enemy artillery fire. The Germans mounted a ferocious counter-attack and the fighting continued until 7 December. For the British the gains had been disappointing, but for both sides the use of tanks en masse brought new strategies and the need to provide greater defences in otherwise 'quiet' sections of the Front.

Above: Post-war photograph showing the extent of the devastation at Cambrai. *Below:* These women are painting the interior of a tank at a British factory. The Mark IV had a crew of eight and was introduced in mid-1917. A total of 1,220 were built in 'Male' and 'Female' variants.

Above: Introduced in 1917, France's Saint-Chamond tank looked very different from the British models and featured a long body with an overhanging front compartment above short caterpillar tracks. Combined with the tank's 23-ton weight, this made it unsuited for traversing difficult terrain. It was armed with a single 75-mm field gun at the front. The Saint-Chamond had a crew of eight. *Below:* A pair of British tanks, with a Mark V 'female', equipped with multiple machine guns, in front of the bigger-gunned 'Male' Mark IV.

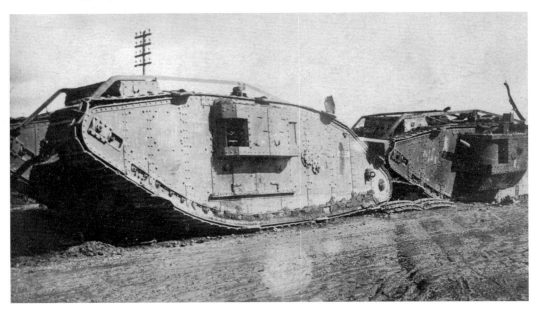

The tanks brought new counter-measures. British troops examine a German Mauser T-gewehr large-calibre 13.2-mm anti-tank rifle. Its recoil was notoriously vicious and could break the user's collar bone or even dislocate a shoulder. It entered production in early 1918.

Above: A Keystone View Company stereoscopic card. 'Down in a shell crater, we fought like Kilkenny Cats – Battle of Cambrai.' These cards were a hangover from Victorian times and, mass-produced, they remained popular as a means of experiencing the action in 3-D.

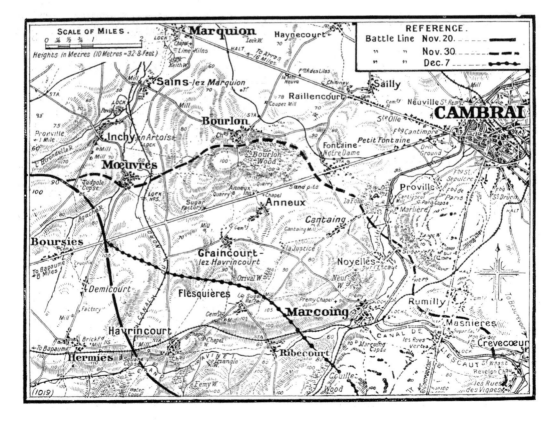

Above: Fireworks in the trenches. These rockets were sent up by the infantry as a signal to the artillery behind the lines. *Below:* British tanks at Cambrai. The one in the foreground has had a section of its side armour removed. This may have been one of the tender tanks.

Above: A rare photograph of the Zeppelin L57. In 1917 this airship was modified in order to undertake an extraordinary rescue mission to Germany's beleagured East African territory. L57 travelled non-stop for almost four days, making a circular trip of 4,225 miles.

Left: This poster by the Maybach-Motoren company celebrates the long-distance flight of the L59. Maybach supplied the engines for the Zeppelins and continued to do so in the inter-war era when the great passenger airships, the *Graf Zeppelin* and *Hindenburg*, plied the transatlantic routes.

The Africa flight of L59

In late 1917 the Germans mounted an audacious rescue plan for the beleaguered troops defending their last African colony, Deautsch-Ostafrika or German East Africa. Under the command of General Paul von Lettow-Vorbeck the Germans had held out against the superior British forces, but they desperately needed ammunition, medical and other supplies. Professor Dr Zupita, the Chief Surgeon of the German Colonial Troops, suggested to the Colonial Ministry in Berlin that a Zeppelin should be sent as von Lettow-Vorbeck was cut off from all other supply methods. Encouraged by a recent long-distance recconaisance flight of the LZ120 over the Baltic, the Navy Minister, Admiral von Capelle, approved the project as this rescue mission could raise national morale, not to mention the prestige of the German Navy. Maintaining possession of at least one colony in Africa might prove to be strategically significant in the event of a peace conference to end the war.

The plan was to send an airship on a 3,600-mile one-way trip from the southernmost airship base at Yambol, in Bulgaria, to Lettow-Vorbeck's garrison at Mehenge, and once there it was to be cannibalised. The framework would be used to build portable barracks, the Maybach engines to run generators, the envelope cut up to make tents, and the gas cell material converted into sleeping bags or clothing, with shirts made from the linen partitioning. The ship chosen for the secret mission was L57 which, along with L59, was a special derivative of the L53 class, modified by the insertion of two additional 49-foot gas cells. Having an overall length of 743 feet (226.5m) and a gas capacity of 2,418,700 cubic feet, these were the largest airships built to date.

As the Zeppelin would not be returning, one of the less experienced officers, Lieutenant-Commander Ludwig Bockholt, was selected to command a crew of twenty-two men. L57 made her first flight on 26 September 1917 at Friedrichshafen, and after a further two trial flights she was sent to Juterborg on the first leg of the trip to Yambol. By 7 October the loading of the special supplies had been completed and Bockholt decided to take the airship from the hangar in order to conduct full-speed trials. Conditions had been calm that afternoon, but as the handling party began to walk her out a side gust caught the stern and threatened to cast the ship against the door frame. Orders were given to get her out of the hangar quickly to avoid any damage and Bockholt took off in haste, anticipating a drop in the wind for a landing towards dusk. When he did land he soon found that the wind had increased and there was little hope of getting her back into the shed, so he elected to take off again to ride out the storm. But the gusty conditions only worsened and at 11.50 p.m. L57 was slammed into the ground. Then, in a momentary lull, Bockholt attempted to bring the damaged airship inside, but she struck the doorway and dragged the 700-strong landing party across the field. Gas was valved when the hull began to twist and break. At 2.00 a.m. the hydrogen was suddenly ignited by a spark and the airship, along with its valuable cargo, was destroyed. Years later it was suggested that L57 had been burned to prevent the secret expedition from being discovered. But the truth is that Bockholt's haste had cost them the airship and any chance of getting the supplies to Lettow-Vorbeck's forces in time.

Resolving to complete the mission to Africa, the Admiralty ordered that L59, which was nearing completion at the dockyards in Staaken, near Berlin, should be lengthened in the same manner as L57 and would be sent in its stead. This work was completed in just sixteen days and on 25 October the L59 made her first flight. On 3 November Bockholt flew L59 from Staaken and over the Balkans to Yambol, with Hugo Eckener on board as a technical advisor. It is said that the special cargo for Lettow-Vorbeck's forces included 311,900 boxes of ammunition, 230 machine-guns, nine spare gun barrels, four infantry rifles with 5,000 cartridges, sixty-one sacks of bandages and medical supplies, two hand-operated sewing machines, three sacks of sewing equipment, mail, telescopes, spare gun-locks, bush-knives and spare parts for the wireless apparatus.

There were two false starts. On 13 November the airship encountered an atmospheric temperature inversion, causing Bockholt to jettison ballast to avoid hitting the hangar, and on the second attempt they were forced back by thunderstorms near Smyrna in Asia Minor. Finally, at 8.30 a.m. on 21 November 1917, the L59 took-off from Yambol with a tail wind taking her south, crossing Turkey and the Sea of Marmora. By 10.15 p.m. that night L59 was off the eastern tip of Crete, where it was engulfed by a thunderstorm. Suddenly the lookout cried in panic through the speaking tube, 'Ship's afire!' A false alarm as harmless St Elmo's fire flickered about the metal parts of the ship. During the storm the radio antenna had been wound back in, cutting off their communications from the powerful radio station near Berlin. Unknown to Bockholt, news had reached the Colonial Office that the British were claiming victory over Lettow-Vorbeck's forces, and it had been decided to recall the airship.

By sunrise the ship was clear of the storm, and oblivious of the recall command, L59 reached the north African coast at the Gulf of Solum at 5.15 a.m. Beneath a cloudless sky the gas began to warm and expand, causing the automatic valves to vent off the surplus, which cost them a ton of water ballast. Having launched in near zero temperatures the crew of L59 were experiencing up to 35 degrees centigrade, and during the day the bright sunlight reflected by the baking sands burnt their eyes and tossed the ship atop thermic columns of rising air. Ernst Lehmann, who was on board, takes up the narrative:

> In the afternoon, there appeared before us the desert city of Dechel with its mosques and multi-storied stone houses. On the horizon the mountains rose like the towers of a fortress, and behind them flowed the mysterious Nile. Until now, everything had gone well on board, but then the gearbox of the forward propeller broke, and in the wireless compartment the operator began to fret over his receiving apparatus.

The L59 continued on four engines, each one rested for one or two hours in every eight. The loss of the forward engine deprived the radio generator of power and they could no longer send messages, although they could still receive them. That night they crossed the Nile in darkness, making a wide circle around Khartoum to avoid being spotted by the British. At around 3.00 a.m. the Zeppelin began an abrupt downward plunge, taking it dangerously close to the mountains, caused by super-cooling of the gas in the humid air of the Nile Valley. With 6,200 lb of ballast and ammunition jettisoned she began to rise again. At 12.45 a.m. the recall message from Berlin finally got through and a despondent Bockholt turned his ship around.

At 3.00 am on the morning of 25 November, the L59 with her weary crew appeared once more over Yambol. She had been in the air for ninety-five hours, almost four days, flying non-stop and covering 4,225 miles in extremes of climate and weather with wide ranges in diurnal temperatures. In the tanks there remained eleven tons of fuel, enough to fly another sixty-four hours or more. It has sometimes been suggested that it was the British who had sent the message to thwart the L59's rescue mission, but this was not the case. Unfortunately for the Germans, the plight of Lettow-Vorbeck had not been as bad as their own intelligence had suggested, but either way the L59 would have reached them too late to have done much good. Even so, the flight of L59 had proven that Zeppelins could travel over long distances, leading to the transatlantic passenger services of the interwar years.

Below: L53 exiting its hangar. The L59 that flew to Africa and back in November 1917 was a special derivative of the L53 class modified for the long-distance flight.

'With the RNAS in the Great War'
During the First World War the lighter-than-air section of the Royal Navy Air Service operated both shipborne kite balloons and non-rigid patrol airships from numerous coastal air stations. These photographs come from a private wartime album belonging to a serving member of the RNAS.

Left: Emerging after an internal inspection of a balloon envelope at RNAS Kingsnorth, on the Isle of Grain on the eastern tip of Kent.

Above: Rigging maintenance at RNAS Kingsnorth. The original caption was: 'At work (a very rare photo).' *Below:* A balloon being 'walked out' out of its canvas-covered shed, RNAS Kingsnorth.

Above: RNAS balloon in flight.

The skeleton
framework of a
balloon shed at
Kingsnorth.

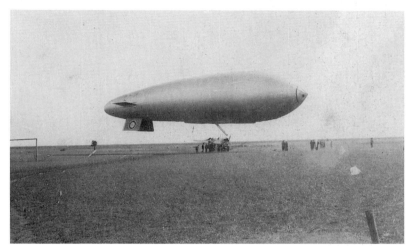

An SS class
non-rigid airship
at Kingsnorth.
A total of 158 of
the Submarine or
Sea Scouts were
built during the war
and they proved
highly effective in
protecting coastal
shipping from
U-boat attack.

A line-up of RNAS
personnel at
Kingsnorth.

Above: Preparing a British aircraft for a night raid on Baron von Richthofen's base at Douai in April 1917. The aircraft is a BE2e, the final variant of the BE2, which was introduced in 1916.

Opposite page, top: The SE5a had a 200 hp Wolseley Viper water-cooled engine. Two guns were carried, a Lewis gun on the upper side of the top plane and a Vickers gun mounted on the fuselage. The latter was synchronised with the airscrew and fired through it. The aircraft's speed was 132 mph at 6,500 feet.

Middle: The Sopwith Triplane was fitted with first the 110 hp and then the 130 hp Clerget air-cooled rotary engine. This gave a speed of 116 mph at 6,500 feet.

Bottom: The French-designed Spad, introduced in 1917. Its name is derived from the Société Pour Avions Deperdussin. It was another single-seater biplane, fitted with the 150 hp Hispano-Suiza engine. Originally it had just a single Vickers machine gun mounted on the fuselage, but on later models this was upped to two guns. Speed was 119 mph at 6,500 feet.

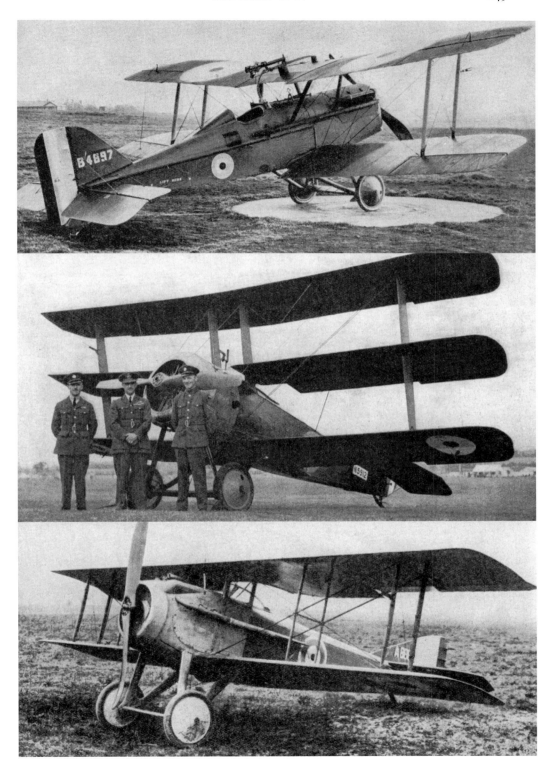

Three celebrated figures from the world of aviation who made the headlines in 1917. Baron Manfred von Richthofen, left, and his fighters of Jasta 11 – the legendary Flying Circus – were causing havoc in the skies over the Western Front. On 7 May, near Douai, they encountered British aircraft of No. 56 Squadron and in the intense dogfight the leading British fighter ace Albert Ball, centre, was killed in a crash landing. In March 1917, Graf von Zeppelin, right, – creator of the rigid-framed airships that bore his name – died at the age of seventy-eight.

A British non-rigid airship, SSZ-59, is shown landing on the afterdeck of HMS *Furious* in May 1918. An aeroplane can be seen on the foredeck landing area on the left of the photo.

DECEMBER 1917

Stuck in the mud! The heavy rains in the autumn of 1917 left many parts of the Western Front as a treacherous quagmire.

On 8 December 1917, Jerusalem ceased to be defended by the Ottoman forces. The following day the Ottoman governor's letter of surrender was given to two British sergeants, James Sedgewick and Frederick Hurcombe, shown above, who had been scouting on the city's outskirts ahead of General Sir Edmund Allenby's main force.

Above: The Mayor of Jerusalem delivers the letter of surrender to the two British sergeants. It stated, 'Due to the severity of the siege of the city and the suffering that this peaceful country has endured from your heavy guns; and for fear that these deadly bombs will hit the holy places, we are forced to hand over to you the city through Hussein al-Husseini, the mayor of Jerusalem, hoping that you will protect Jerusalem the way we have protected it for more than five hundred years.' The decree was signed by Izzat, the Mutasarrif of Jerusalem. *Below:* German and Turkish prisoners are marched out of the city.

Above: British artillery enters Jerusalem, hauled by American-built Holt 75 half-tracks. The later versions of these were built without the front 'tiller' wheel. *Below:* The Jerusalem to Kantara railway. The first British trains reached Jerusalem on 27 December 1917.

General Sir Edmund Allenby entered Jerusalem on 9 December 1917. He proceeded on foot through the Jaffa Gate as a mark of respect for the holy place.

In the advance and Battle of Jerusalem the Ottomans suffered over 25,000 casualties and 12,000 men and 100 guns were taken prisoner by the British Empire forces. *Above:* German prisoners being transported by truck. *Below:* A group of Turkish prisoners.

Designed for use inshore and in shallow waters, the Insect class gunboats were originally designed for warfare on the Danube but at least four served their early careers on the Tigris and Euphrates in Mesopotamia. *Cicala* spent part of her career in White Russia, on the River Dvina, and was sunk by Japanese bombs on 21 December 1941.

The important Russian town at Vladivostok was occupied from 31 December 1917 by British, American and Japanese navy vessels. With Japanese imperialist expansion, it was necessary to prevent them having full control of the port.

On the Home Front. *Above:* Crowds greet wounded soldiers returning via Charing Cross station in London. *Below:* An enthusiastic reception for the veterans of Mons, on their way to a special event held at the Albert Hall on 15 December 1917.

Coal. In 1917 all coal mines passed into the possession of the Board of Trade to ensure that the production and supply of coal were maintained, both for domestic users and for the war industries. *Top:* Soldiers distributing coal from an Army lorry in the winter of 1917. *Bottom:* Children carrying home the family coal supply.

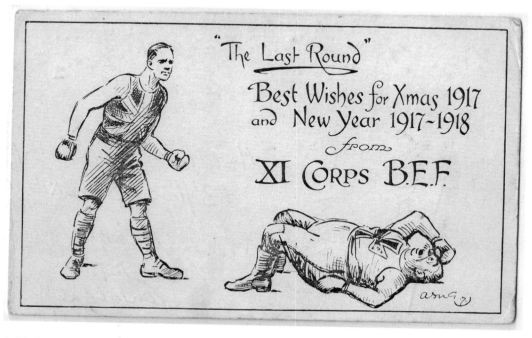

A Christmas card from XI Corps of the BEF, looking forward to their last round with the Germans. It would come by November 1918, when the guns would finally fall silent on the Western Front.